Flights of
Fancy

Flights of Fancy

**Stories, Conversations and Life Travels
with a Bemused Columnist and His Whimsical Wife**

*Randy Fitzgerald
, /21 /20*

*(and
Barb ♥)*

Randy & Barbara Fitzgerald

BEACH GLASS
BOOKS

Published by Beach Glass Books
Design and composition by Ray McAllister
Printed and manufactured in the United States of
America
First printing 2017

Library of Congress Cataloging-in-Publication Data
applied for

Randy Fitzgerald 1941—
Barbara Fitzgerald 1941—
Flights of Fancy: Stories, Conversations and Life Travels
    with a Bemused Columnist and His Whimsical Wife
    / by Randy Fitzgerald and Barbara Fitzgerald
ISBN 10: 0-9987881-2-8
ISBN 13: 978-0-9987881-2-8

This book is dedicated

To All the Readers

who, for almost 30 years, have called, emailed, shown up at our speeches, or written cards and letters to comment, discuss, critique and share their thoughts and feelings with us—but mostly to offer friendship and kinship, which we return in kind.

Contents

Contents

Foreword

Finally, I have stopped being amazed by the reaction to Randy Fitzgerald.

It took awhile.

I couldn't quite figure how this completely unassuming man received not only tons of fan mail but also received rapt attention from roomfuls of adoring readers—yes, adoring.

Women, mostly, it seemed.

Yes, women.

Randy *gets it*, of course. He's both understanding and perceptive, as any good columnist should be. More than most. And funny, yes. Very funny. Droll.

But he's a teensy bit devious, you see. Maybe it's just that he engages in misdirection. He hits us with surprises, but he also shifts the ground on which we're walking. This, for instance, is how he begins one column:

> You be the judge. Here's the story. Let's say there's a wife—could be anybody's wife, you understand— who ordinarily works from home but who has temporarily taken on a full-time job that keeps her at

a desk on the other side of town all day. This new responsibility prevents the wife from keeping the house, especially the kitchen, up to its usual standards of straight/neat/clean.

Maybe this unknown wife's unknown husband who, heaven knows, would generally be out there helping with the straightening/neatening/cleaning is at a very busy time at his own job, so ...

It's the "so" that signals we're starting our flight. Fasten belts for takeoff. By now we know he's not talking about just any husband, nor an unknown wife. He's talking about himself and his own wife, Barb.

Doesn't matter. We're about to be reeled in by a simple story of what will turn out to be a simple mistake—really, hardly even a mistake at all—that, yes, in hindsight, could have been avoided. He'll be taking the blame ... yet he's also hinting that he wasn't the only one to blame, not really, not if you look at it fairly. ...

Isn't that a bit devious? ...

And soon we realize, wait a minute, he really *is* writing about any husband and wife. About Everyman and Everywoman. He's writing about *us*. No wonder we're hooked.

Wow, he is devious.

By then, we're smiling, laughing—and making so many knowing nods our necks hurt.

I got to know Randy when we both were writing columns for the *Richmond Times-Dispatch*. Newspaper columnists get fan mail, but Randy got the type normally reserved for— let's not overstate this—*ELVIS*!

Barb showed me some. A couple excerpts:

- *"With every column I read, I say to myself, 'I must write Randy and tell him about how his words touch my life,' but I never have, until today. Thanks for sharing your life with us all."*

- *"I don't make a habit of writing to newspaper columnists—I do love your column, though. Have been reading it for years and am often moved to both laughter and tears."*

Foreword

- *"Thank you for always capturing your readers' feelings and writing just what we are feeling but don't know how to put into words."*
- *"The column was hilarious. Sounds like our household. Were you looking in our window to get some ideas for your story?"*

To set the record straight, no, Randy was not looking in anyone's window.

At least I don't believe so.

Years later, when I'd left the paper to write books and also began editing *Boomer* magazine, I grabbed him to write for *Boomer*. Readers there immediately loved him, too, filling our mailbox—which by then was an inbox. He was honored as Virginia's best magazine columnist

One thing I realized then was that Barb was an integral part of his columns. It wasn't just that she frequently appeared in them. Her *voice* could be heard in them. Randy, it seems, often bounced ideas off her. He incorporated Barb's view with his. Their crazy life was a crazy *shared* life. Maybe that's what you get when you've each been married three times—twice to each other. (OK, I said they were perceptive. Not sane.)

Why hadn't he put out a book of columns? I asked. I can't remember what Randy answered—I'm sure it was self-effacing; you know how he is—but we filed away the notion. By 2017, I had left *Boomer* and, while writing my books, begun publishing other authors. We resurrected the idea.

So here it is, Randy's long-awaited book of columns, which is actually Randy and Barb's long-awaited book of columns, which is, more accurately still, their continuing conversation about their travels through this crazy life. The columns have been culled from several publications, supplemented with family photos and Douglas Payne's very fine illustrations. Randy and Barb have interspersed background, follow-ups and observations from today, too. It's an autobiography of sorts—with them sitting in the room with you.

Offer them some chips and a drink, why don't you?

FLIGHTS OF FANCY

Publishing *Flights of Fancy* has been a joy. The book is funny and knowing. It's also, I should note, poignant from time to time. It can be painful. If you don't feel the occasional lump in your throat, well, check your pulse.

But you'll love it. Randy *gets it*, you see. Barb does, too.

Oh, and Randy is devious.

I've warned you.

Ray McAllister
Richmond, Virginia
August 2017

Preface(s)

On March 2, 1988, a new columnist appeared in *The Richmond News Leader*, his debut piece a recounting of stories from a Richmond Forum appearance by the top Soviet journalist of the day, Vladimir Pozner.

Sadly, the new columnist did not resist the opportunity to say "A funny thing happened to Pozner on his way to the Forum," but he did include a good joke about the speaker and the KGB. Precedents for storytelling and humor had been set.

As this book is being prepared for press, that columnist—the one pictured alongside the column back then with a unibrow and a full head of dark hair—sits down the hall polishing up his regular column for *Boomer* magazine, still writing after all these years.

More than 2,000 columns bear the Randy Fitzgerald byline. They have been published in more than half-a-dozen area newspapers and magazines over the past 30 years, under various column names: Close to Home, Second Thoughts, The Time of My Life, One Man's Family and By the Way. With so many columns and so many deadlines, imagine the lies he must have necessarily told!

Over the years Randy has also written several thousand news and sports articles in area papers, including Richmond's *News Leader* and *Times-Dispatch*, as well as the *Daily Progress* in Charlottesville. But it is his folksy and funny columns that have captured the fancy of local readers since that first one appeared in '88. He is primarily a humorist, but many of his best stories have been tributes to the downtrodden, the troubled and the victimized.

Randy's own days became troubled in late 2016 and early 2017 when, just at the time he began assembling copy for this book, he suffered a heart attack, followed two months later by a stroke. While he lost his peripheral vision and is still a bit wobbly, his sense of humor, unibrow, and ability to defeat his bride at Jeopardy remain intact.

To make Randy's life easier as he recovers, I—his bride of indeterminable years—took over readying this book for publication, adding copy and chapter introductions at his request, writing a bit myself and accepting his kind offer to name me as co-author. It seems to be my one chance to have my name on a book and, obviously having no pride, I accept.

Barbara Fitzgerald

*U*ncle Roy used to say "These golden years are hell." Uncle Roy, a recurring character in many of my columns over the years, may have been right, but from my recent perspective, every day is golden. I am mending now from the heart attack, a quadruple bypass, an aortic valve replacement and a stroke, and I expect to be back in good shape before long. At the moment, though, I'm afraid Mr. Trump would have to tag me as, at best,

Preface(s)

"low-energy Randy." Despite a certain lack of focus these days, I have made occasional contributions to this book under the clever pseudonym of "Randy."

In compiling the book, Barb and I have occasionally changed, modified or omitted things that originally appeared in certain columns, like political or topical references that no longer make sense all these years later, but most of the columns are intact as they first ran.

My good wife (hereinafter "Barb") has done basically ALL of the work of pulling this book together, but her involvement in these columns started long before my health problems did. She is a writer herself, running her own small copywriting and public relations shop, WordsWorth, since the early 1990s. Over the years, she has many times suggested column ideas, provided the perfect last line, written a better lede or come up with just the right word when I'm looking for it. Many times I've told stories almost word for word as I've heard her relate them to others. She's been my editor, proofreader, often co-writer and, always, my muse.

I cannot explain to you how it is possible that she can be all those things and yet also be this absolutely ditzy woman I write about who chases burglars down the alley barefoot, packs a lunch to follow the cat in order to see where he spends his day, backs the car over my Martin guitar, and spends $125 on adult lingerie at the age of 70. I always say I'll never run out of material as long as I'm married to Barb. Between her marvelous sense of adventure and my notorious jerk gene, it's an interesting life. I welcome you to it.

Randy Fitzgerald

On August 6, 1986, you're invited

to the University of Richmond

to witness a natural phenomenon

that will occur no more than twice

in your lifetime. It last happened in

August 1961. If you missed it then,

don't pass up a second chance.

James Randolph Fitzgerald and

Barbara Goodman Fitzgerald Colvert

cordially invite you to their wedding

at Cannon Memorial Chapel at 7:30

on Wednesday evening, August 6, 1986

(the 25th anniversary of their first marriage).

Celebration party to follow at their home.

Sometimes a second chance is just in the stars.

CHAPTER ONE

Our Story

BARB: *The strange course of our romance and relationship may be helpful in understanding some column references, as well as accounting for the humor and the empathy in Randy's writing.*

Besides, it's my love story and I like to tell it.

Sharing "Our Story" has been my assignment at the speeches we've been giving around town for years, and it's a good place to start this book of columns that in many ways have served as a journal of our marriage and of one man's family.

Our Story

By Barb

*R*andy and I met our senior year in high school in the fall of 1958—a regrettable, even disgraceful, time in the history of the Commonwealth of Virginia. That was the year the state's governor, J. Lindsay Almond, chose to endorse the Massive Resistance policies of Virginia's powerful segregationist senator, Harry Byrd. Rather than allow federally mandated integration to take place, Gov. Almond closed down Lane High School in Charlottesville that year, along with schools in Front Royal and Norfolk.

While his classmates from Lane High were educated under a national spotlight that fall in makeshift classrooms in churches and community buildings all across the city of Charlottesville, Randy and his family had fortuitously just moved into neighboring Albemarle County, making Randy eligible to attend Albemarle High his senior year—my school, as it were.

So even our first meeting was not without a dramatic story line, along with a hint of inevitability. Our senior year we became good friends and colleagues. I edited the school paper, and he was the sports editor. We shared a speech class, and I gave a speech about him. We called each other nearly every night, talking into the wee hours of the morning, trying to avoid detection by our sleepy-eyed mothers. We double dated to senior prom—but not as each other's date. We were by then best friends.

Off we went to college—Longwood for me, the

Our Story

University of Richmond for Rand. We wrote weekly letters sharing our college experiences. On weekends, he would bring a carload of fraternity brothers down to Longwood, and I would find them dates. (I had first choice.) One cold night near the end of freshman year, I was a girl short, and Randy and I ended up crammed in the back seat with two other couples, with me on his lap. We married at the end of our sophomore years, on August 6, 1961.

For the next 15 years, one or both of us were either in college or teaching at one. We shared English majors and pursued more degrees and careers as professors. We lived and taught in Georgia, South Carolina and back home in Virginia—and then in England and Wales for a spell. During the '60s, we focused on political activism and Randy's Ph.D. We never had the children we wanted, but we had a marriage so good that a friend once said, "If something ever happens to you two, I'll stop believing in love."

Something happened.

The process was gradual and sad, but the worst happened. We grew apart and could not find our way back. Randy says that once that first marriage hit a rough spot and was no longer perfect, we couldn't settle for less. So we separated and, a few years later, divorced.

During our 10 years apart, we remained friends. We had lunch. We loaned each other money. We both gave up teaching—I went into advertising and Rand to public relations. But we continued to share what was going on in our now-divergent careers and lives. Eventually we both married other people and had the children we'd never been fortunate enough to have together. But we continued to wave as we passed.

When I was a few months shy of 40, I had a daughter, Sarah. And when Rand was 40, he had a son, Kyle. We showed off our babies to each other, I passed Sarah's baby bed along to Kyle, and then I moved to Dallas. Thereafter, communications were limited to baby pictures and Christmas cards.

Those marriages did not work out, and in 1985 Randy's sister, my dear friend Linda, (along with her 3-year-old son, Jed) came to Dallas to visit me. Upon learning that I was getting a divorce, she shared that Randy was getting a divorce, too, and that I should call him as he'd never been as happy as when we were together. I felt the same way.

Soon we were calling each other every night, after we had put our children to bed, and talking long into the morning hours, just as we had done in our high school years.

In March of 1986, I moved back to Richmond with Sarah, and Randy and I remarried on August 6 of that year—the day that would have been our original 25th anniversary. This time, our marriage has been air-tight. As Randy once wrote in a column, "It was always clear to us that the stakes were higher than during our first childless marriage. This union brought with it the custody of Barb's 5-year-old daughter and my 4-year-old son. Both children already had been through one divorce in their short lives, so Barb and I came into that chapel knowing we were going to be family for the duration."

Beyond that, of course we still loved each other. We wanted it to work for us, too, and we determined from the start that divorce would never be an option. This year, we celebrated our 31st anniversary—or, if we can add the two marriages together, our 46th. Sometimes we count our 10 years apart as just a sabbatical and add that missing decade back in, too, as though it never happened. Each year on August 6, Randy gives me three presents. And, this time around, every day together is a gift as well.

BARB: *Our story also appeared in the October 1997 issue of Good Housekeeping. (You can find it in your doctor's office.) This is Randy's column about that article, slightly abridged to avoid repetition with "Our Story" above.*

15 Minutes of Fame

I have only one question: What was she thinking?
That's what I asked Barb when I first heard that *Good Housekeeping* was going to publish our love story.

"Well," she happily chirped, "someone called and asked to tell the story from my perspective, and it seemed like a good idea. It's our 15 minutes of fame."

Here's how it came about. Apparently someone connected to *Good Housekeeping* made a request online early this year for couples who had been married, then divorced, and later remarried happily.

We think a reader of the column sent in our names. Once the writer called and Barb filled her in on a few of the details, we ended up as October '97 playmates of the month.

"Did you notice," I asked Barb, "that the article is called 'My Problem and How I Solved It,' and that the word 'Problem' falls dramatically right over my forehead? And why did you feel it necessary to mention that during our years apart, I—and I quote— 'dated one woman after another'?"

"All part of the story," she explained. "I did take pains not to refer specifically to the one with the buck teeth, though. And you'll find only a passing reference to the snake handler."

From the *Richmond Times-Dispatch,* Sept. 3, 1997

my problem AND HOW I SOLVED IT

Left, Randy and me on our wedding day, August 6, 1961. *Right,* the two of us today—older and definitely wiser.

"*I Couldn't Forget My Ex-Husband*"

We'd been divorced for almost a decade, but when Randy called, I felt an overwhelming urge to see him again. Should I give my first love a second chance?

by Barbara Fitzgerald as told to Sondra Forsyth

The night we decided to separate, it was warm and dark, with barely a sliver of a moon over McIntire Park in Charlottesville, VA. We walked silently, side by side, toward what had been our special place the summer we'd fallen in love. We were drawn back to that spot after 15 years of marriage, as if the magic of the setting might somehow make things right again. But it didn't. I sat on a swing, and Randy started pushing me higher and higher, just as he'd done when we were young and full of dreams. For a long time, we didn't speak. There was nothing left to say that we hadn't already said about trying to make our marriage work. Finally, Randy stopped pushing and the swing slowed. We both knew it was over between us. For nearly three years, we'd been growing in different directions, and now it was as if we were almost strangers.

I choked back tears and said, "Maybe we should try it apart for awhile."

Randy nodded slowly and said, "I guess it's better not to have anything at all if we can't have what we had."

It was hard to say good-bye to something that had once been so beautiful. Our romance had begun during our senior year of high school when I was the editor in chief of the student newspaper

good housekeeping/October 1997

and Randy was the sports editor. We were soul mates from the start, laughing at the same things and getting into heady discussions. After graduation, we went to different colleges, but saw each other on weekends. By our sophomore year, we were engaged. We got married the summer of 1961, and our friends said that if we ever split up, they'd quit believing in love.

We were a team, friends as well as lovers. We both worked our way through college and graduate school and then spent a glorious year in Europe while Randy researched his dissertation. When we came back, we created a cozy life on a little farm, that my father owned outside of Charlottesville. We both worked as substitute teachers, and we didn't have much money. But we were happy, growing and canning vegetables, getting around on a purple motorcycle. We talked about having kids. Eventually, Randy got his Ph.D.

In those days, there was a glut of Ph.D.'s, and Randy couldn't get a job as a professor. So, at the end of that first year, he took the best stopgap job he could find: mailman. I found work as an office temp. We tried to make the best of it—we'd come home with funny stories about attack dogs and crazy bosses. But looking back, I realize that year was the

turning point. Nothing was happening the way we'd planned. Randy didn't have a job in his field and I didn't even have a field. We'd been trying to have a baby, but we'd made no progress there either.

We tried everything from temperature charts to short-term abstinence. No luck. Whenever we'd baby-sit for our friends' kids, we'd feel sad and envious. Randy wanted children just as much as I did. We talked about the possibility of going through the whole battery of tests for infertility, but I'm kind of a fatalist and felt that if we were meant to be parents, it would happen naturally. It never did.

After awhile, we just stopped talking about it. The loss was there, though, hanging in the air. Then, finally, Randy got a teaching job—at a campus in Petersburg, 90 miles away. That's when my grief over not getting pregnant really intensified. I felt as though I had nothing. Between temp jobs, I rattled around the farm feeling useless and bored. I was angry sometimes too. Certain things about Randy suddenly started to irritate me. Why was I picking up his dirty socks and wet towels? Why was he so extravagant? I tried talking to Randy about my frustrations a couple of times, and he was sympathetic, but that didn't change the fact that he had an outside life and I didn't. *(continued on page 80)*

RIGHT PHOTOGRAPH BY MARK ATKINSON

GOOD HOUSEKEEPING, OCTOBER 1997.
PHOTOGRAPH AT RIGHT BY MARK ATKINSON

Our Story

"This article makes it look like I didn't work much," I said, quoting again: 'In those days there was a glut of Ph.D.s and Randy couldn't get a job as a professor.' What about all those years I taught at Georgia and the College of Charleston?"

"Nobody wants to hear about that," she replied. "A story has to have a certain amount of dramatic tension to work."

"Well, I'm feeling the tension," I noted. "What do you have to say about this line? 'Why was I picking up dirty socks and wet towels?' Gee, Barb, must we air our dirty linen in public here?"

"That would be wet linen," she said. "Besides, that happened the first time we were married. This time you rarely leave your things on the floor."

"Something I learned in later relationships," I admitted. "Never leave your clothes on the floor when you're dating a snake handler."

"I must ask," I said to her, "are you going to be comfortable with Aunt Mary and the preacher reading about our futile attempts to have children during that first marriage?"

"That part actually did worry me, and it was there that I made my only copy change," she said. "I had them take out the term 'sex life.' No one wants to see the words 'sex life' alongside pictures of a 55-year-old couple. I'm still not sure what the kids will think about this article."

So we called our two teenagers into the bedroom, and Barb spoke to them.

"Sarah, Kyle, your dad and I are going to be featured in an article in the next issue of *Good Housekeeping*, and it's going to tell all about our marriages and our family, and it mentions both of you by name. I thought I'd better warn you."

Sarah, who is 16, looked around the bedroom, taking in the dirty socks and wet towels on the floor, and delivered her honest opinion: "The Fitzgeralds are going to be in *Good Housekeeping*? Now that's ironic."

7

CHAPTER TWO

Reader Favorites

RANDY: *In 1990, Valentine's Day completely got away from me. I forgot the flowers, forgot the candy, forgot the card. (That lapse may have been the first indication of a previously undiagnosed male jerk gene.)*

From that year forward, Barb took charge of Valentine's.

For more than 25 years thereafter, she has made reservations, usually at a romantic bed and breakfast somewhere in the state, driven me there for an overnight date, brought along presents, and arranged dinner at a nice restaurant and a proper celebration. I never know where we're going until we get there.

But in 1991, it did not appear that either of us would be able to get away to celebrate our special day. This column (which appeared a year later) recounts her efforts to plan a memorable Valentine's Day for us.

Her Heart Was in the Right Place

My wife will have to go some this year to beat the Valentine's surprise she came up with in '91.

Like so many busy couples these days, particularly ones with young children, Barb and I often go for several days at a time passing like ships in the night. I'm off on one of my three jobs and she's juggling a bunch of freelance writing assignments, and the children have to get to basketball practice or the dentist or another birthday party.

So Barb and I kiss each other hello and goodbye and smile and wave as we pass until one of us finally says, "Gosh, I've got so much to tell you. Can we sit down and talk?"

February a year ago was a case in point. It was one of our busiest months, and when we started to try to make plans for Valentine's Day, it just wasn't working out.

I was scheduled all that day for a conference at the Jefferson Hotel, and Barb was interviewing somebody that evening for an article. It was going to be a long day and a late night.

The only compromise we could find was that Barb agreed to join me and my public relations colleagues down at the Jefferson for lunch. It would definitely be a business occasion, a buffet, maybe even with a speech or two. Very romantic.

After my round of morning meetings, I met Barb in

From *The Richmond News Leader,* Feb. 12-13, 1992

that beautiful Jefferson lobby. She was all gussied up and beaming. As I directed her towards the banquet room, she said, "No, wait. First there's someone I want you to see."

On the way upstairs in the elevator, she told me she had run into columnist Guy Friddell earlier in the lobby. Guy is a favorite columnist of ours who writes for the Norfolk paper, and he had invited us up to say hello.

I was more than happy at the prospect of seeing Guy again and feeling pretty darn good about being invited up. When we got to the room Barb had indicated, Guy did not answer my knock. But the door was ajar and, to my horror, Barb just pushed it open and went in.

You can imagine my surprise when I saw my slippers under Guy Friddell's bed.

Guy was not there, of course, never had been. But what was there was a table set beautifully for lunch, complete with flowers, candles, a card and gifts for me, and a silver bucket with a bottle of champagne.

Within moments, a scrumptious lunch arrived at the door from the restaurant downstairs, and we ate leisurely and privately, delighted to have stolen an hour or so for ourselves in the middle of 20th-century American mayhem.

Barb had me convulsed with laughter as she described her arrangements and her arrival. First she had called and asked the Jefferson folks if they rented rooms by the hour. Without blinking an eye, they told her that they did not, but would she be interested in half a day?

She would indeed, if that was the only way she could get a room for lunch. But she said she did feel a need to explain to the desk clerk that she was bringing her husband there as a Valentine surprise.

No doubt the nice lady who took her reservation believed that one-hour lunch story right up to the moment Barb arrived at the front desk with a huge suitcase.

It was loaded down with the champagne, the silver bucket we were given as a wedding present, a tape player with my favorite music and, "for a homey touch," my slippers and our own hand towels and silverware.

Barb said that when she put the suitcase down on the floor at the desk, it clanged so loudly that the clerk actually leaned over to take a look at it. "It sounded exactly like chains and handcuffs in there," said Barb.

The desk clerk began to look at the 50-year-old matron in front of her with new respect.

The lunch was splendid. And I was very impressed that Barb had spent for one hour the kind of money it must have cost to book a lovely room at the Jefferson, even at the half-day rate. She's usually much more practical than that.

Along about 1 p.m., Barb started packing up and said it was time to go. "Oh, I can be a few minutes late," I said. "What's the hurry if you paid for half the day?"

"Well, actually," my wonderfully romantic wife confessed, throwing things madly back into the suitcase, "the only way we could afford this is that I sublet the hour from 1 to 2 to your brother and his wife."

BARB: *Randy told the story of making a complete disaster of our home in several publications over the years. He also explained it three times on the phone to the insurance company and more than once to the good people at the clean-up service.*

Hurricane Randy

*B*arb and I had considerable damage to the house during the recent storm days, but most of it was caused not by Hurricane Isabel but by another damaging force altogether.

That very Thursday afternoon as the whole city anxiously awaited the arrival of the dread Isabel on our doorstep, I took pains to follow all the good advice I was hearing on television about storm preparations. First, the helpful announcer said to fill up the bathtub with water, in case power went out, so I went in and got that process under way. Then he said to bring in flower pots and secure lawn furniture, and I did both of those.

I checked the flashlight and radio batteries, I filled water jugs in the kitchen, I moved the cars from beneath trees.

While I was handling all these important details, Barb was in bed, recovering from a bad cold she had caught shortly before we had been evacuated from Nags Head two days earlier because of another storm.

When all the precautions had been taken for Isabel, I stretched out across a bed in the guest room, not wanting to

From the *Richmond Times-Dispatch*, Oct. 1, 2003

wake Barb, and dozed off for a couple of hours myself.

When I awoke, I heard water furiously rushing, close at hand. I remember thinking, "Isabel is here early, and it sounds like the gutters are already down."

As it turned out, she wasn't, and they weren't.

Now that I was awake, the nightmare began. A few steps into the hall showed me that the flood I was hearing was not outside the house but inside, and it suddenly came to me with great clarity that, some two hours earlier, I had turned on the water in the bathtub and forgotten to turn it off.

Oh, the tub was well-filled at that point, believe me, as were the two hardwood floors in bedrooms on either side of that bath, the living room ceiling beneath those rooms, the living room floor and, as I soon discovered, even the basement beneath all that.

What to do? Where to start? I grabbed as many towels as I could carry downstairs and began sopping and mopping in the living room, but even now with the water turned off, it was like operating in a rainstorm as water that had backed up in the ceiling continued to pour onto my head and into the various buckets, pots, pans, bowls, vases and wastebaskets I had distributed around the room.

DOUGLAS PAYNE

Soon I ran out of towels and moved up to bedspreads, sheets, quilts and random articles of clothing, which I spread all over the floor, only to have them almost immediately saturated, too. (Barb has since been telling people that I even got poor Lucy Dog's blanket and tossed it onto the heap, and all I can say about that is that she wasn't using it at the time.)

Speaking of Barb, about a half hour into my futile clean-up efforts, I heard her weak and perplexed voice at the top of the stairs, no doubt having heard something akin to the James River coursing through our parlor. "Randy?" she said, cautiously.

"Don't come down here," I instructed her. "Don't come down." But she did, of course, and her reaction stunned me as much as had my earlier discovery of Venice's Grand Canal between the sofa and the piano.

First she gasped. Then she laughed. I had expected the gasp but certainly not the laugh. She told me later that I looked so distressed and pathetic that she hadn't wanted to make me feel worse. Besides, she always has in the back of her head the motto her mother had often called up in irreversibly bad situations: "You might as well laugh."

"Why didn't you call me to help?" she asked.

"I was afraid to," I admitted.

Eventually, of course, the ceiling stopped leaking. You may recall from a column earlier this year that it had been newly plastered; now it hangs in strips, and yellow water stains decorate the side walls. But the towels and spreads did their job, to dry on the clothesline during the next seven days when we were without power. (That was Isabel's fault, not mine.)

The basement got the worst of it. Not only did the ceiling tiles collapse there and the water pretty much destroy everything it landed on, but Isabel did her part to flood everything from the floor drain up as well.

Isabel also took a gutter and shingles off and broke a lot of tree limbs, but at least her work is covered by insurance. We're not sure about my own efforts as yet. When Barb called the insurance company to see if our coverage included husbands who overflowed the bathtub, the agent said, "Has there been a Hurricane Randy I haven't heard about?"

I think that I should at least qualify as a tropical storm.

14

Cat
Tales

*A*fter a virtual lifetime of championing women's rights, I lately have been revealed as a secret male chauvinist.

I had the first glimmer of this realization several weeks ago when my wife, Barb, came into the study to point out that the kittens—one male, one female—we found in the alley back in the summer were nearly of an age to be neutered.

"Boy, they really grew up fast," I observed. "When are you taking her in?"

Barb, who had started out of the room, turned back. "What do you mean 'her'?" she asked. "I believe this is a matter of 'them,' isn't it?"

"Well," I reasoned carefully. "If we did 'her,' we wouldn't have to do 'them.'"

"Wait a minute," said my ordinarily agreeable wife. "Are you saying you have hesitations about getting the tom-cat neutered and none about having the female spayed?"

I had to think about that and, well, yes, that was exactly what I was saying.

My logic was that good old Muffin Cat was going to actually look different if he were neutered. For the rest of his life, this noble animal would face the ignominy of having perfect strangers come up and say, "Oh, isn't she beautiful!"

Whereas the female's limitations would be considerably less obvious to the world.

So I explained all this to Barb, albeit a good deal less delicately than I'm explaining it to you.

From *The Richmond News Leader*, January 17-18, 1990

"Maybe," I said, "they could do something a little closer to a vasectomy on him and not so much the elaborate procedure I've got the problem with."

So Barb got on the phone to our vet. "No, Mrs. Fitzgerald," she was told in what she thought was a carefully controlled voice fighting off laughter. "We don't do vasectomies on tomcats."

So while she had the vet on the phone, she made the appointment for neutering and spaying.

Upon hearing the news, the female cat, Nibbles, very wisely immediately went into heat, thereby postponing her surgery for several weeks, but poor old Muffin Cat still had a date with destiny.

Frankly, I found it very hard to talk with him in the days before his surgery, especially after we received in the mail from the Cat Clinic a cheerful, brightly colored reminder with a drawing of a smiling Cheshire cat.

It said, "It's time for Muffin to come to our clinic for . . ." and then there was a list of things that might have been checked, like feline distemper or leukemia vaccine.

The box that had been checked was "Other," after which someone—it looked to me like feminine handwriting—had actually written in the dread word "castration."

The night, when Muffin came to my chair purring, I tried to give him my "It's-for-your-own-good" speech.

"Let's see if I've got this right," he said at one point. "Nibbles goes into heat so I have to make the ultimate sacrifice, is that it?"

"Well," I said, "actually, the operation will help you stay close to home and not get hurt in fights. And it also will help us keep the house smelling nice."

"Oh," he said, sarcastically, "why didn't you say that to start with? If you had just told me it was all so the house would smell nice, why, I would have suggested castration myself."

Then he gave me the dirtiest look I've ever received

16

from a cat and left the room.

When the day arrived, I didn't want to know anything about it. In fact, I had pretended not to see the big note Barb had left in the kitchen the night before. "No food or drink for Muffin after 6 p.m."

At work the next day, I received a call from Barb at 4 p.m. "Muffin's ready," she said. "Will you pick him up, since you're already in the West End?"

I didn't want to do it. That's probably why it took me 50 minutes to get from the University of Richmond to Gaskins and Broad. I made two wrong turns and settled into Innsbrook traffic heading the wrong way.

When I got to the clinic, they had Muffin in a cage, ready to go. "He did fine," the vet said. "Call us if you have a problem."

Wondering if she had meant me personally, I hurried out the door with a very subdued cat in a cage.

It's now several days later, and Muff is indeed fine. In fact, I think his sexual identity is intact, even if my smart-aleck wife did say she's noticed he has a new fondness for quiche.

BARB: *One of Randy's readers wrote him a note after the previous column appeared and said Randy had guaranteed that Muffin would suffer exactly that fate from the day he allowed him to be named Muffin. After that note, our nickname for him became Moe.*

The following column ran 17 years later, in 2007.

There are a number of columns recounting the misadventures of Muffin and his ill-fated sister, Nibbles, in the intervening years.

Digging Up Memories

Moe lay in the grass and watched us dig his grave.

His eyesight wasn't as sharp as in days past, and he was having trouble holding his head up, but to the end, despite the fact that all his organs and systems had broken down, that he had been on IV fluids for four months, that his quality of life had passed the point of any good return, he managed a few last moments of cat curiosity in our direction.

The only way Barb had gotten through the morning, knowing it was the last day in the life of a pet we had loved and pampered for almost 18 years, was alternating tears and gallows humor. As she took her turn with the shovel under the clothesline, she looked over at Moe, so bony and frail, who once had been the biggest, longest, heaviest tomcat in the neighborhood, and she said to him, "I'm planting begonias here, Mr. Moe."

From *The Community Weekly*, October 29, 2007

And then a moment later she answered herself, as she has for years in the voice I recognize as Cat: "Wrong season for planting, Miss Barbara."

Very wrong season. There may be a time to love and a time to die, but there is never a season when it's easy to bury a beloved pet. No matter how much you can see that they are at—or even beyond the point they need to be put down—it's a hard, hard thing to do.

Barb and I have fought this decision all summer. This cat was our last pet standing, and for the five years since our children grew up and moved away, our baby. He had outlived his sister cat, found alongside him under a neighbor's garage in the summer of '89, both having been dropped on the city street from a passing car. They were so tiny and young that their survival was in doubt for days. Barb nursed them along with hand feeding and love, and when the kids came home from summer camp two weeks later, they found they each had been granted a kitten in their absence.

They named them Nibbles and Muffin, the female a calico and the male a gray with a snow-white vest and paws and a black Hitler mustache. He was a roughneck. He'd fight any cat that turned up in his territory, and many a time he limped home with a slashed face and a bleeding paw. Once he ran headlong into the side of a passing car and never stopped moving, returning home hours later with knots and scrapes from the car door, walking stiffly but with eight lives intact. He would need them all.

He was such a dog-like cat, meeting me at the car when I came home from work, putting his front paws up on my knee, waiting for his head to be petted. He would almost always run away from you instantly after swatting your leg or overturning a vase, hiding until the moment had passed. He didn't wait for you to yell—he was gone before you could react. Very smart cat.

On the morning his sister Nibbles was killed a few years back by two neighborhood dogs that came upon her as she slept on our front porch, Muffin had been exiled for just that kind of affront. Maybe he had put a paw in the birdcage or jumped onto a kitchen counter, but on that day Barb had deposited him in the basement and slammed the door. That may have saved his life. Nibbles, who never left the yard, was outside alone. After the chaos of that morning—the growling and snarling of the dogs, the screams of Nibbles and then of Barb as she rushed out the front door, the confusion as neighbors gathered in the yard—Barb saw Muffin in the basement window, watching the whole thing, eyes wide.

After that day, once Nibbles was buried under the same clothesline where Muffin was destined to rest, his personality changed. He never hissed at us again, never swatted or scratched and never was as enthusiastic about leaving the house. He was appreciative from then on for every kind word or the touch of a hand. He wanted to sleep in the bed with us at night and stay close to our heels by day.

He still wanted to be near, at the end as we dug his grave. Barb and I took turns digging, and when the rock and roots and sadness became too much, our neighbors Tom and Karin came and took over the job, and we retreated with Moe onto the back porch to await the vet and say our goodbyes.

No more pets. This is it. In our time together Barb and I have buried three dogs, three cats and two birds. No more. Saturday was too hard a day. And Moe was just too good a cat.

 **BARB:** *In 2012, we took in daughter Sarah's two black cats when she moved to Wyoming and couldn't transport them. They are lovely cats—but when I look up from my computer, it's a picture of Muffin I see, fast asleep on our bed and stretching from one side almost all the way to the other.*

To this day, I have never been able to reread the column Randy wrote in September 2003 about Nibbles' horrible death.

Family Album

This seems an appropriate place for some happier photos. Readers often ask to see family members.

RIGHT: Randy turns his back on his family, or possibly they all turned their backs on him. Left: brother-in-law Joel and Randy's sister, Linda. Right: brother Terry and sister-in-law Frances.

BELOW: The Fitzgeralds: Daughter Sarah, her fiancé Ian, Randy, son Kyle . . . and Barb photobombing them all.

RIGHT: Lucy Dog, the rat terrier who starred in many a Fitzgerald column, bounds along the Rappahannock River in her glory days.

21

RANDY: *This particular story was a legend in the family long before it became a column. In fact, the first time I wrote about Thanksgiving 1993, I had to leave out the best part because Barb was too embarrassed to share it. But some 10 years later, I went back and told the rest of the story. It was ultimately just too good not to share. We can't recall now where that second part of the story appeared and could not find it as we prepared this book. But here's the first part, which appeared in December 1993, and then Barb will tell you the rest of the story.*

Dressing for Thanksgiving

Regardless of what you've been told, there is a perfectly simple explanation for why I happened to be wearing a big black cardboard Pilgrim hat with a yellow crayon buckle when I ran into former Virginia Governor Gerald L. Baliles on the front porch of the Rodes Farm Inn at Wintergreen on Thanksgiving Day.

And anyway, I didn't look any stranger than my wife in her cardboard bonnet and collar or my nephew Jed in his construction paper headdress, complete with chicken feathers.

Each Thanksgiving, from 14 to 20 members of my family set off for a couple of days together at some interesting place where there is an excellent chance of a fantastic turkey day meal that none of us had to cook. This year,

From the *Richmond Times-Dispatch*, December 1, 1993

Wintergreen was blessed with the Fitzgerald contingent, and we were all a little punch-drunk to be away from home and together.

My teenage niece Tiffany showed up with handmade head garb for the whole clan to wear to dinner, everything from a feather or two on a cardboard band to a chieftain's headdress to the elaborate Pilgrim stovepipe that I was wearing.

Naturally when someone has gone to the trouble to create actual artwork accessories, the least you can do is look like a total idiot and clamp it to your head, which we all did. Who could have predicted that Baliles and his distinguished party would turn up in the same waiting line for dinner?

Thankfully, Baliles doesn't know me from Miles Standish and actually gave my unseemly party a little smile and wave, indicating that we should all go in before him—a move both kind and wise. I mean, would you want a party of 14 wearing cardboard hats at your back? Me neither.

RANDY: *That was part of the original column about that Thanksgiving. The rest of it described some other activities we undertook during that visit to Wintergreen.*

But here's the part of the story that went unshared for a decade, as told by Barb, the guilty party herself.

"It's All Gravy"
By Barb

Like most families, we Fitzgeralds love Thanksgiving leftovers, and that's the one trouble with a Thanksgiving dinner away from home. There's nothing to eat at 9 o'clock on Thanksgiving night when you're back in your room, craving a turkey sandwich with a little dressing and a touch of cranberry on the side. To solve that problem, I decided that for the 1993 Thanksgiving, I would take along several sandwich bags in my purse and save for later whatever portion of dinner could be spared. The problem was, this was a buffet dinner and take-out doggie bags were probably not encouraged. I won't go into the take-out misdemeanors of others in the family, but let me just say that, at the end of the meal, after I had already appropriated several slices of turkey for late-night feasting, my eye fell upon the gravy boat conveniently located on my side of the table. I promptly opened wide a big plastic bag in my purse and poured what was left of the gravy directly therein.

I glanced up to see the horrified reaction of my sister-in-law Frances, who had been informed of the turkey take-out plans but was understandably confused to see me pouring gravy into my nice leather handbag. And if she was confused, you should have seen the look on the face of the governor! Yes, when I glanced around to see who else might have been watching, I met the interested eyes of the former governor of Virginia, the honorable Gerald Baliles.

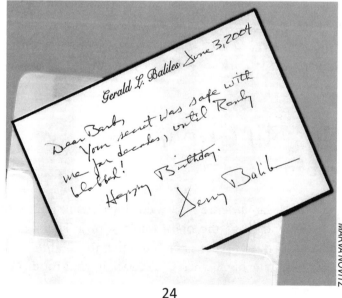

MARVA NOVITZ

The leftovers were delicious that night, and the gravy-in-the-purse legend was born. As time went on, I figured that the statute of limitations had run out on gravy crimes, so I told Randy he could now tell the full story, which he did in 2004 in a column we now can't find.

I know it appeared in 2004, though, because of a letter that came to the house in early June of that year, shortly after that follow-up column must have run. Inside was a brief note that said, "Dear Barb, Your secret was safe with me for decades, until Randy blabbed." It was signed "Jerry Baliles."

CHAPTER THREE

Our Favorite Columns

RANDY: *In preparing for this book, Barb and I went through, I'm pretty sure, thousands of columns crammed into boxes and file cabinets around the house, and at least once a day in the middle of the search, one of us would say, "Oh, here's my favorite column!" So obviously we have a lot of favorites between us.*

Choosing "your" favorites was not too hard, because those were the ones people most often mention when we're giving speeches or bring up when they run into us somewhere. They're also the columns that got the most letters from readers. The three that follow are our favorites today, but don't hold us to it. Our choices may be different tomorrow.

MARVA NOVITZ
On a hotel rooftop in Cannes, 55 years after,
and a very LONG way away from Fayetteville.

BARB: *You will notice that the column below appeared one day after the 10th anniversary of our second wedding—I considered it my favorite gift that year. Sadly, I misplaced the little strip of wood somewhere along the way, I think at the point I sent the secretary out to get it refinished. I find myself still looking for it here and there, even many years after it disappeared.*

'I Promised You'

More than 25 years ago, Barb and I became heir to a piece of furniture that is well over 100 years old. It is a cherry secretary 5 feet tall with glass-doored, floor-length bookcases on either side and a drop-front desk in the middle, attached by two thick brass chains.

The decorative brass on the piece is extraordinary, with swirls and scrollwork so elaborate it seems almost an Oriental piece. There are ornate brass handles on either side, for aesthetic purposes, no doubt, because there is no way in the world two men lifting, one on either end, could get this thing off the floor. We've moved it a half-dozen times, and anyone who has helped has always begged for a chance to carry the piano instead.

This beautiful piece of furniture has been in Barb's family for years, passed around a little and eventually ending up in Uncle Roy's barn up near Charlottesville. There Barb spied it in 1970 and proclaimed her love.

It was a big hassle getting it to Charleston, S.C.,

From the *Richmond Times-Dispatch*, August 7, 1996

where we then lived. With the help of every brother-in-law I could round up, I finally got it loaded into a rental truck, drove it 400 miles down busy old state Route 17, and unloaded it with the help of five friends and neighbors.

As soon as it was in place in the living room, Barb polished its brass and wood until it gleamed, and then we sat down together on the sofa to admire it. As we gazed proudly, we saw something black and spindly legged crawl quickly from behind it and dart across the wall. It was a black widow spider, transported all the way from a Virginia barn to a South Carolina condo. It was not the last surprise this piece of furniture would yield.

Years went by. Before we knew it, Barb and I had been married 10 years, then 12, then 15. And then, before we knew it, the marriage broke up.

The parting was sad and hard for both of us. We remained friendly, though, and delayed divorce for several years after. Finally, though, we signed the papers, married other people, and eventually had the children with others that we'd always wanted when we had been together.

Fast forward a few years. When both those marriages broke up, Barb and I got back in touch and remarried each other 10 years ago yesterday, on Aug. 6, 1986. Had we stayed together the first time, that day would have marked our 25th anniversary.

So yesterday Barb and I were married for 10 years the second time—or, if you add the first 15 to the current 10, a total of 25 years, with a 10-year sabbatical in between.

During our years apart, I had kept the secretary because Barb had moved to Dallas and didn't want to transport it all the way there. But with our remarriage, she was delighted to have it (and one would hope, me) back.

The night we moved it into our new home together in '86, Barb polished the secretary once more. And in the process, she discovered something that had eluded us for all those years. Behind one of the small drawers in the piece was a small secret slot that contained a surprise far more pleasant than a black widow spider.

There we found a small strip of wood, two inches long and maybe half an inch high. And into the wood were burned the words, "I promised you."

Those simple words spoke clearly to Barb and me— to two people who had not been able to live up to the promise they had made each other years earlier. But we promised ourselves anew that night that this time, we would stay married forever, working our way through whatever came along.

In this past decade, I've thought many times about the fellow who carved those words. What had he promised her? That they would be wed? That he would be faithful forever? That he would return from war? That they would get back together?

Or maybe he simply promised he would someday carve with his own hands a beautiful bookcase from the cherry tree in the yard, to hold their copies of Dickens' novels, which he would read to their children by the fireside at bedtime.

The little piece of wood remains in its hiding place now, but the thought we carry with us. Promises made are meant to be kept, are meant to be powerful and strong enough to hold families together, to guarantee children both their parents, to see people through rough spots and to teach the value of commitment and honor.

I am grateful to the man and woman who left us that reminder. This time, we won't forget.

BARB: *As you move from my favorite to Randy's, please note the difference in tone between the loving, sentimental choice of the wife (above) and that which a male judges to be a great column. Here's a favorite of Randy's.*

Tales from the Bedroom

*A*fter all these years, it has come down to this: the old girl and I just can't continue to share the same bedroom. One of us will have to go.

All you other baby boomers out there know what I'm talking about. Once you get into your 50s, it gets a lot harder to sleep soundly through the night. The slightest little thing will wake you up after you're 50, and once you're awake, you're often awake for the duration. That's when sharing the bedroom gets harder and harder.

I'm not saying it's always her fault. Sometimes she's sleeping perfectly quietly and, if I get up for a pill I forgot to take or for a trip down the hall, I'm the one to wake her up. Then she's up roaming around the room at all hours, fooling with the cats or doing heaven-knows-what in the closet.

Some nights she goes in the study adjoining our room and stretches out on the sofa, but it's colder in there and I worry about her getting sick. Yet I must admit, we both seem to sleep better on those nights when she's in one room and I another.

Somehow when you get older, sleep gets not only a lot harder but a lot noisier. I've noticed that as she ages, she's

From the *Richmond Times-Dispatch*, May 1, 2002

snoring a lot more. Heck, I probably am, too, but she's also making a bunch of strange little noises I've never heard from her before—a little whistle in her breathing or a little cry out. But it's the snorting that really gets to me.

She seems to be breathing a lot louder lately, too. The heavy breathing alone is enough to wake me, but if I wake up on my own and can't hear her breathing, then I lie in the dark in dread until it starts up again.

Sometimes she groans a little—I guess that's her arthritis talking. If I can stretch my foot over there on her and give her a little nudge, she'll settle down briefly, but usually she's back to making strange noises before I can get back to sleep myself.

I hate to admit this, but for my own sanity I had to evict her from our bed last year. It was a hard thing to do. We've shared a bed and a room for a lot of years, but I finally just had to conclude that separate beds were the best thing for both of us. I just couldn't take her restlessness and noisy sleep any longer, and no doubt she was tired of my rolling over into her space and waking her up as well.

Nevertheless I could see she felt bad about it at first, but probably no worse than I did. I saw her in the dark standing at the side of the bed for a long time that first night after I turned out the light, and I felt rotten about not inviting her back in. But I had to get up in the morning and go to work and she didn't, so I pretended I didn't see her there.

Having her in her own bed alongside mine did alleviate a lot of our sleep problems for awhile, but lately I'm tuning in more to her night noises and we're waking each other up a half dozen times every night.

I just haven't been able to bring myself to ease her out of the bedroom. I have some friends who've made that call, but they've felt guilty about it afterward, and it's not something they talk about much. Last night, when she started up with the little high-pitched whine in her throat, it was the last straw. I tried to talk her awake.

"Hey, baby," I said. "Wake up now. Wake up."

But ironically, while my turning over in bed can bring her wide awake and often to her feet in seconds, her hearing is getting so bad that I really have to raise my voice for her to hear that.

Finally—and don't think I'm proud to admit this—I took off one of my socks, rolled it into a ball, and tossed it gently her way. I think I must have scored a direct hit, because she leaped up in surprise and gave me—I saw in the moonlight—one of the dirtiest looks I've ever gotten.

Then it was really all I could do to get back to sleep. She got back in her own bed, but along about 3 a.m. she had her revenge. She started chewing on her feet so loud, gnawing and slurping, that she even woke up Barb.

"Randy, is that the dog or you?" Barb asked sleepily.

"It's the dog," I said, with resignation.

I know you're going to think less of me for it, but tonight Lucy Dog's bed gets moved out into the hall. That old dog is 15 now, or well over 100 in dog years, and her nighttime problems are only going to get worse. On the other hand, so are my own, and since I'm a believer that what goes around comes around, perhaps I'd best let sleeping dogs lie.

~⁓~

A Honeymoon a Bride Won't Forget

Now that it's June and officially the month of weddings, I offer as a community service some valuable counsel to any young man out there who may be contemplating the big step.

This advice may seem simplistic and even obvious but ignore it at your peril.

Do not under any circumstance plan your honeymoon around a trip to Fayetteville, N.C., "the Putt-Putt Capital of the World."

That is what I did 33 summers ago at the unworldly age of 19, and I have yet to live it down.

I can tell you now that if you honeymoon there, whatever you do that's romantically imaginative for the rest of your life, your wife will never let you live down Fayetteville.

You can be floating down a canal in Amsterdam 20 years later, singing, "Isn't It Romantic?" in your best Sunday baritone, and she will interrupt you to observe, "Well, we've certainly come a long way from Fayetteville."

Or you can be ensconced on your anniversary in palatial quarters at the ultra-expensive Grove Park Inn in Asheville, perusing a menu featuring squab and spotted grouse, only to hear the light of your life point out that this part of North Carolina is sure a step up from Fayetteville.

Oh, I admit I made a dumb, dumb decision back then, but like so much in life, you have to put it in context. You must know that I had spent every spare moment that

From the *Richmond Times-Dispatch*, June 1, 1994

spring and summer of 1961 on L. F. Wood's Putt-Putt course in Charlottesville, training and preparing for the weekly summer PPA (Professional Putters of America) tournaments.

I lived and breathed Putt-Putt for months. Sometimes L. F. would leave the lights on for me, and I'd play by myself half the night.

I planned, you see, to finance a wonderful honeymoon for Barb and me after our August wedding with my winnings, which surely would mount up over the summer. I did have a summer job at the local Biffburger as well, but that money was already earmarked for college and moving expenses for the newlyweds. Whatever I earned at Putt-Putt was gravy—and honeymoon.

The short version of the story is that I actually was the leading money winner that summer, wining about $300, as I recall—a fortune to a young man in those days. All that remained was to plan the honeymoon.

I don't know if grooms still make that decision by themselves and surprise the bride, but in my day that's how it was done. When Fayetteville occurred to me as a destination, it felt so right I almost leapt up.

After all, wasn't Fayetteville the very place where Putt-Putt had been invented? That place where devotees of the game could still play the very first course in America? A town with not one but numerous courses to choose among? And since Putt-Putt was making the trip possible, wasn't it romantic to visit the home of Putt-Putt for the honeymoon?

Apparently it was not.

As we drove away from the First Presbyterian Church in Charlottesville and headed south, Barb had no idea what lay ahead for her. "Florida?" she guessed. No, my dear, it will be far more exciting than Florida.

"Atlanta," she ventured, as we continued south. I actually hooted. Why would anyone want to honeymoon in a big, hectic city like Atlanta?

When we rolled into Fayetteville and stopped, I think

it's safe to say that never in her wildest imagination had Barb considered it as our destination. She recovered nicely, however, pointing out that the truck route on which we found our motel had lovely flowers in the median. She's always been able to spring back quickly.

But as years passed, I gradually learned what she truly thought of that amazing honeymoon in Fayetteville. Suffice it to say that we have never revisited.

In fact, the second time we got married, in August of '86, I headed us off in the opposite direction. We flew

DOUGLAS PAYNE

to Boston, rented a Caddy, and drove all the way up the coast far into Maine. We stayed at old inns and B&Bs, visiting Salem and Kennebunkport. We shopped at L. L. Bean and strolled rocky beaches.

It was spectacular. And Barb was good enough not to bring up the past, though as we drove by a Putt-Putt our first night out, she did turn to me with a smile and say, "Don't even think about it."

Shoes Make the Man

"**B**y the way," Barb said when I got home last Wednesday. "Kyle had to wear your shoes to school today."

Apparently I had left for work with our son Kyle's shoes in my car, and it being chapel day at Luther Memorial School, he had to quickly come up with some replacements from my closet.

Barb could have had no idea of the impact of her seemingly insignificant words on a dad, but my response was so pronounced that I actually went and sat down to think about it.

My 13-year-old son fits into my shoes? How is that possible? Aren't those the same little feet that hung around my neck such a brief time ago, when I used to carry him on my shoulders at the mall and in the park? How long ago was that first step, anyway? Wasn't it just a short time since I stopped tying his shoelaces?

Now, apparently, all the little piggies have gone home. My boy slips into my shoes and heads out to junior high.

Ah, my dear son, don't you be in such a hurry to wear the shoes of a grown-up. Before you know it, you'll be trading your tennis shoes for wingtips, and your life will never be the same.

Will I be swinging in a glider somewhere when you're hurrying through a hundred airports in your Florsheims, grabbing a shoeshine where you can on your way from Duluth to Toledo, working to climb that ladder and accomplish whatever it is we men are supposed to achieve? Success?

From the *Richmond Times-Dispatch*, May 17, 1995

Wealth? Self-worth? Admiration? Hang on to those Reeboks, my boy—it's not an easy world out there.

How long before you inherit that American work ethic that leaves men feeling responsible and sometimes overwhelmed with the pressures of supporting a family, even when there's a wife working just as hard alongside? Will you be able to balance the demands of supporting yourself and your family with a job you truly enjoy? I wish that for you with all my heart. It's so important because for many, job becomes life.

You're so laid back you may just settle into a comfortable pair of worn boots and go off in your own direction, sending me a postcard occasionally from Jackson Hole or Taos. Or maybe it's work shoes you'll be needing as you undertake some honest labor that tans your face under a hard hat and leaves you in such good shape that your old dad won't be so eager to roughhouse with you anymore.

I refuse even to consider the spit and polish of shiny black military shoes in your future. God forbid that in your time there will still be muddy battlefields out there waiting to mess up the shoes and lives of your generation, as happened to my own. I don't want to be naïve, but perhaps—I hope—we will be leaving you a better world than that.

If your own 13-year-old dreams come true, it will be cleats on your feet in your first job, won't it? For you share the baseball reveries of many generations of men, your own dad included. We're the ones who prefer to hang on to some part of the boy we once were.

Is there a chance you'll be rich and wind up with real Italian leather on your feet, heels never run down or turned over? That would be nice if you want it, but I must tell you that if it comes, you'd be the first in the family on Easy Street.

On the other hand, if you're already in my shoe size at 13, maybe you're going to far outstrip your old man. Maybe you'll be bigger and bolder and better, and that's OK with me. I'm going to get another shot at life just by watching you. I've already started that, and it's a joy.

As I think about what lies ahead for you, Kyle, out there in my shoes somewhere, a short piece of advice, if you don't mind: RUN. Head in whatever direction you want in this life, but run. Time is short. One day you're a boy, turn around and you're a man.

Run hard. Give life all you've got, live it well, live it fully. Find the things and people important to you, and go after them with your whole heart.

I remember—oh, yes—what it was like to be 13. Everything is ahead, all of life's beautiful, difficult, uplifting, deflating, mysterious, confusing, exhilarating, wonderful experiences. What a journey lies ahead! And from the perspective of being 53 and so far on the other side of it, I must say I wouldn't mind at all being in your shoes.

'Come Back and See Us, Y'hear'

few months back I made some passing comments here about a seeming decline in sanitary standards at some of Richmond's famous and not-so-famous eating establishments.

The column inspired a number of letters and calls from readers with horror stories of their own, but I will resist sharing them with you so that we all may continue to eat out with innocence and pleasure.

But their stories led me to my favorite dining-out story, which should be no surprise to my readers since everything leads me to a story.

Finding a restaurant for breakfast after church is always a problem for my family. The good ones are always crowded and the wait is long, or you end up with a brunch menu and the cost is great. Or we like a place but the kids don't, or vice versa.

So a few months back I was overjoyed to see a review in the newspaper of an absolutely splendid place in the Fan District for a late family breakfast. I can't identify the establishment for obvious reasons, but after you hear my report, you won't be heading there in droves anyway.

First off, there was only one waitress on duty covering the whole restaurant, a middle-aged woman who yelled across to us as we arrived that we'd have to wait. Our little family stood very patiently, talking quietly among ourselves, happy to be the only ones in line.

After a few minutes, a couple at a table near us got

From the *Richmond Times-Dispatch*, January 19, 1994

up and left, and soon another party stood and left shortly thereafter. On both tables were only menus and glasses of water. The waitress came hurrying out of the kitchen just as the retreating guests went out the door and came over to us in a snit. "Why did they leave?" she asked, accusingly, looking long and hard at our two perfectly behaved children.

When I ventured that perhaps they grew tired of waiting, she said, "Well, if some of you lazy people would stay home on a Sunday and fix your own breakfast, I wouldn't be so overworked here and maybe the service would be better."

Barb, the first among us to get her voice back and her lips moving, defended us and the other customers (the seated ones) rather cheerfully, I thought.

"After church," Barb said in friendly fashion, "I like to continue to be with my family rather than having to go in the kitchen and cook a meal."

And the waitress gave her a scathing look and said, "Did it ever occur to you that some of the rest of us might like to go to church, too, but we have to be here waiting on people like you?"

At that point our gracious hostess led the way through a now very quiet and subdued restaurant, seated us, and said helpfully, "Whadda you want?"

It occurred to me that perhaps the food critic who had reviewed this place had come in with a nametag saying, "I am the newspaper's food critic." Or perhaps he visited on this woman's day off. Or maybe he was an investor in the company.

Anyway, Barb ordered her usual eating-out breakfast—her weekly egg, hash browns, toast and, when a restaurant has them, a side order of grits.

Our meals arrived about a half hour later, and the grits were missing. When Barb finally caught the waitress's eye and inquired about them, a look of disbelief came over the woman's already-unhappy face.

"Wait a minute," she said loudly enough for all in the establishment to hear. "You ordered both hash browns AND grits?" Then she turned to the next table, presumably having recognized them as people who would know and frown upon a pig when they saw one. "Whoever orders hash browns AND grits? How much starch does a body need? And look at that! She actually has buttered toast, too."

Had she been a man, I would have had to crack an egg on her head at that point, but this lady was clearly out there somewhere the buses don't run. Before I could say anything, Barb and the kids started laughing. I mean, it was so outrageous and impossible that all you could do was laugh.

When a few of the other patrons joined us in our incredulous mirth, shaking their heads and laughing with us, the waitress stomped off to get grits. And here's the part you will definitely believe because I know it's happened to you after lousy service. When Miss Congeniality returned at the end of the meal with our check, she was all sugar and bonhomie. "I'm so sorry you had to wait for your grits," she said. "Come back and see us, y'hear."

Having grown up in my family's restaurant business, I have always felt that not tipping was a felony. So I'm embarrassed to tell you that I could not walk out of that place without leaving a few dollars on the table.

But as we left, Barb, who had worked long and hard as a waitress herself when we were in graduate school, enhanced my minimal gratuity by depositing upon it a big buttery spoonful of grits.

BARB: *This was the second column Randy wrote, back in 1988. I remember he came home totally exhilarated from having met and interviewed one of his musical heroes. "I think I'm really going to enjoy this column-writing thing," he said. The column remains one of his favorites. Bill Monroe died in 1996.*

How Can He Play So Fast, Sing So High?

*T*he metallic bus is parked in the Cock 'n Bull's parking lot on MacArthur Avenue on Richmond's North Side. On its side is painted "Bill Monroe and the Bluegrass Boys."

Wayne Lewis, a former Bluegrass boy who now has his own band, has driven the bus from Nashville for the show tonight, and now he is bringing its famous owner his dinner.

I had arrived just moments before, so Bill Monroe and I talk as he eats his chicken wing dings and onion rings, compliments of the owners of the nightclub. Monroe, 76, is the father of bluegrass, a country string-band music named after his home state of Kentucky. Bluegrass music features mandolin, banjo, guitar and fiddle and close vocal harmonies. It can lift your spirits and make you want to get out there and dance, or it can break your heart and make you want to cry.

Monroe is a man of few words and a lot of nods— and, in response to a question, he is likely to limit himself to "yessir" or "no sir." Not an easy interview, but an impressive presence.

From *The Richmond News Leader*, March 9, 1988

43

"My health has not been too good this past year," he says. "I've had some heart problems. Been eating too fast. People say I ought to retire." Before the night is over, he will have played two sets, mingled with admirers and headed on the bus back to Nashville sometime after 1 a.m. He has ridden on this bus and others like it for more than 50 years, averaging 150 to 200 days on the road every year.

The bus is really more an RV than a bus, with plush bench seats lining one wall, a breakfast nook on the other and a color television wedged in the corner. "Alf" is on, with its orange-haired, big-nosed extraterrestrial star, and Bill yells at Wayne as Wayne is heading out the door: "Come back here. There's someone on this show that looks just like you." But Wayne is gone in search of a non-caffeinated drink for his former boss.

The Cock 'n Bull often packs them in on Fridays with house band George Winn and the Bluegrass Partners and on Saturdays with a number of other local groups, like the Hanover Better Boys. But tonight is clearly special with the appearance of the man who started it all in the 1930s and who helped produce such musicians as Lester Flatt, Earl Scruggs and Mac Wiseman. There are pictures on the walls of these men and others who have played here, at Richmond's only real bluegrass nightspot.

Shortly after Winn has started his set, Monroe walks in the front door, shaking hands as he heads toward the pool room to await his own show time. The pool table is covered with Monroe tapes, albums and other memorabilia, all for sale.

From my vantage point at the end of the bar, I can see the show out front and Monroe in the back.

Monroe takes a chair in the pool room and begins warming up on his mandolin. People keep coming over to shake his hand, ask for his autograph and to pose for pictures with him. He warmly greets them all. He is royalty in this place.

"How fortunate we are to have our good friend Bill Monroe with us tonight," Winn says to the crowd. "All the bluegrass you hear, no matter who plays it, it stems back to Bill Monroe."

Two aspiring fiddle players, who brought along their fiddles, gather around Monroe's fiddler, Mike Feagan, who is also warming up. Feagan amiably plays music with them.

Monroe begins his trek from the pool room to the stage when Charlotte Parsons, tonight's promoter, takes him by the hand. On stage, he breaks into a spirited "Blue-Eyed Darlin' " and welcomes his audience. "Hidy, hidy, hidy, hidy," he shouts. He no longer looks 76, and retirement seems out of the question.

Then his fingers fly over the mandolin break for "Old Home Town." And when he gets to "Muleskinner Blues," you have to wonder how he can play so fast and sing so high.

Monroe finishes with a rousing "Rawhide." He salutes and heads off stage for a little more socializing before he hits that old long, lonesome highway, one more time.

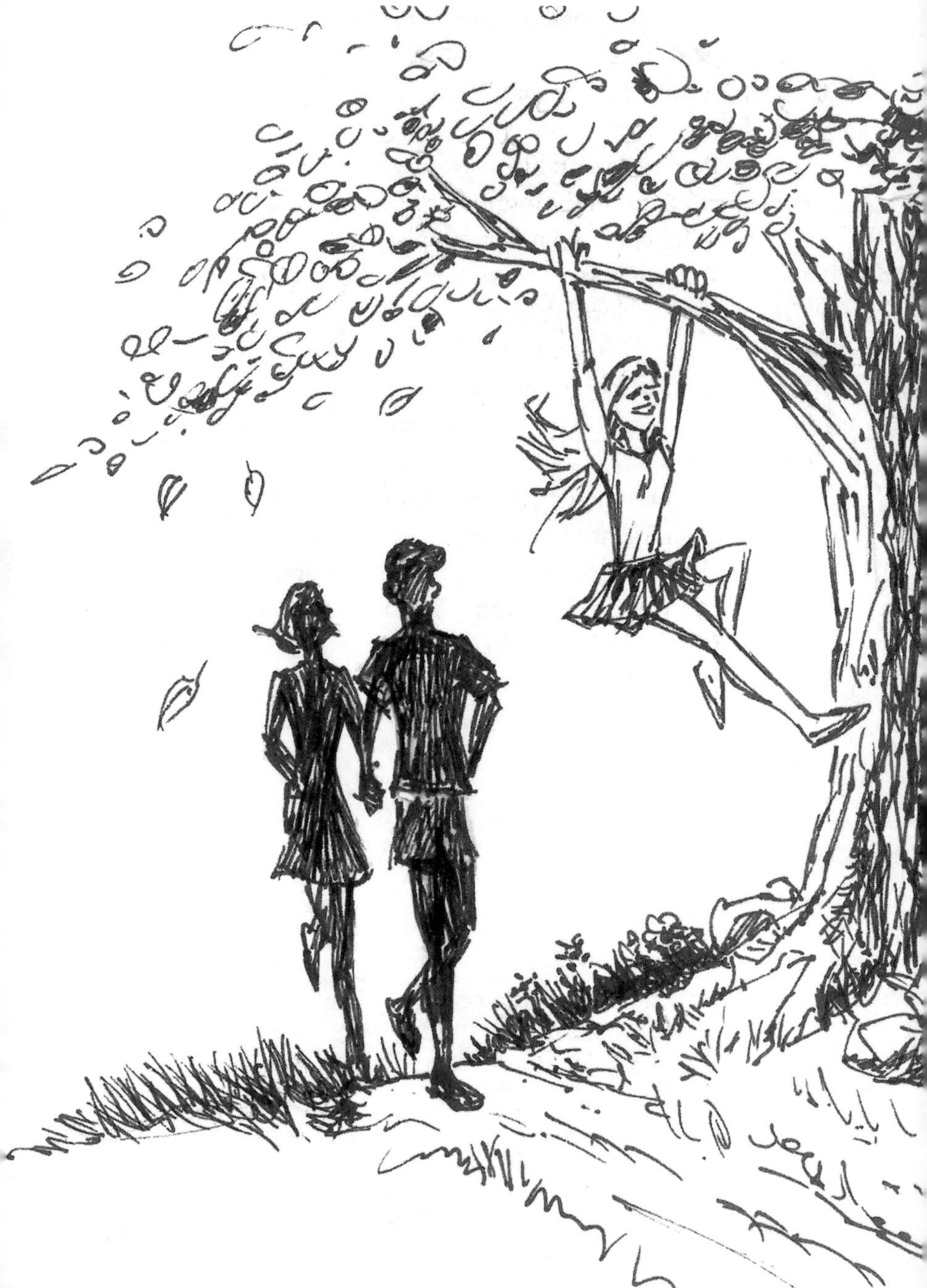

BARB: *This vignette is excerpted (and shortened a bit) from a column Randy wrote in 1999 on, of all things, the jerk gene. I'm not sure how this story fit into that topic, but after it ran, he heard from several men who had married the girl in the tree and several women who WERE her.*

Choose the Girl in the Tree

On Sunday morn, I walked over to the track at the hospital and watched from a distance as a young woman climbed a tree. I smiled to behold her the way one might smile at a babbling brook or a morning glory. She was one of the beautiful gifts the world occasionally provides for jaded eyes.

She was about my daughter's age, I think, and when I first saw her, she was walking with two friends who were obviously a couple.

As I watched, she caught sight of a low branch on a maple tree and, in one graceful move, swung up onto it

From the *Richmond Times-Dispatch*, November 10, 1999

DOUGLAS PAYNE

and disappeared among red and gold leaves. I could hear her laughter ringing among the branches, all lightness and youth and sheer joy of living. I couldn't wait to get around the curve of the track and bring the little group back into view because I knew something about the scene was speaking to me.

When I could see them again, the girl was high up in the tree, her green shirt appearing and disappearing among the red and gold like some last vestige of summer leaf, darting and dodging to avoid the inevitable transforming hand of autumn.

The boy below was making a half-hearted effort to climb the tree himself, but he was more a linebacker than a tree climber and wasn't up to the leap of faith it took to swing up over that first limb. I sensed that he was too afraid of failure to give it a try.

Go for it, I wanted to tell him. Go up after the girl who climbs trees. Go for the risk taker, the limb swinger, the one looking for a special vantage point from which to view the world. The girl with a laugh like Christmas bells on a sleigh. You can't go wrong with a girl like that.

The scene evoked a memory for me of 30 years past, of an afternoon Barb and I had spent on The Battery when we lived in Charleston in 1969. That was the year Neil Armstrong walked on the moon, the troubled year of Chappaquiddick and the Manson family. It was still very much Vietnam, too, a time when the next day could bring only more of the unexpected.

Barb and I walked that day in the park that looks out over the two rivers, talking of worldly cares. In the middle of a thought, with no warning, Barb kicked off her shoes and swung up into a tree. "I'm getting above it all," she said, and I swung up beside her.

It makes no difference that a policeman came along a few minutes later and made us get down. Nobody gets to stay above the world for long. There are just too many lost keys and bad wars, too much broken porcelain and too many broken promises.

But in the end a girl who climbs trees is too busy looking toward the sky to let life get her down. That's the girl you can't let get away.

CHAPTER FOUR

Barb

RANDY: *Now that we're telling Barb stories, I got a million of 'em. Some were just vignettes, not enough to fill a whole column, but over the years I managed to slip them in whenever I could.*

Like the time Barb and her sister Rue were in the funeral procession for their Aunt Mattie. The two sisters had not seen each other for several weeks and were soon deep in conversation as Barb drove them toward the cemetery in a long line of family and friends. Somewhere along the way Barb forgot where she was and started passing the other cars. She passed the immediate family. She passed the preacher. She was gaining on the hearse when Rue suddenly took note and reminded her that they were in a funeral procession.

It reminded me of the story of Auntie Mame in the fox hunt as she passed all the other riders, then the dogs and was gaining on the fox.

Here are some stories of my own Mame!

Barb sings along as Randy strums his beloved Martin guitar
at the log cabin in Galax. The guitar later had a memorable accident.

❦

'O, what a tangled web we weave, when first we practice to deceive'

—Sir Walter Scott, speaking of my wife, Barb

OK, I need the best advice you can give me. Things have not been what they've seemed for almost two months at my house. During all that time, Barb has not been telling me the truth about her comings and goings. In fact—there's no nice way to say this—she has been flat out telling one lie after another.

Every Wednesday night she's been gone for a solid hour and a half, ostensibly taking a quilting class from the County of Henrico Recreation and Parks. She'd return with a bounce in her step and a smile on her lips, with a radiance that one wouldn't normally associate with quilting.

"I didn't know you wanted to learn to quilt," I observed. And she replied, cool as a mountain breeze, "Oh, but I do. And Laura and Katie from work are taking it as well."

So as any one of you husbands out there might have done, I went back to reading my paper and said, "That's nice, dear."

Weeks passed. Sometimes I would ask her questions, taking the appropriate interest in her pursuits. "Are you sewing by hand or machine?" I asked one night. And she replied, smoothly, "Oh, they have machines there for us."

I pursued the point. "I wouldn't have thought there'd be sewing machines at an elementary school?" And as quick as you please she said, "They bring them in just for this class."

Some nights she'd come home and drop quilting terms on me, like "batting" and "squares" and "pieces." One week she was "learning the stitch"; another she was working on a "sampler quilt."

I didn't even wise up when her friend Laura made a big mistake. One Wednesday when Barb had gone to visit her sister Betts for the afternoon, Laura turned up at my door after work with a brown paper bag. "I have to miss class tonight," she said, "so here's Barb's veil." Then she got a horrified look on her face, and when she returned to her car, I thought I saw her beat her head against the steering wheel a few times before she drove away.

The bag held a gauzy, filmy fabric like nothing I've ever seen on a quilt before. Even a man who can't wield a needle well enough to remove a splinter could see that.

When Barb got home with minutes to spare before her class, I said, "Laura dropped off the veil you need for class tonight."

And with only the slightest, almost imperceptible, pause—oh, this woman is good!—she said, "Wonderful. I'll need that. It goes between the squares and the batting." And off she went.

Last Saturday night, finally, the extent of her deception was revealed. I had been out on a hot golf course all day, coming home exhausted at dusk. When I drove up, the house was dark, but the living room was full of burning candles. The smell of incense was in the air, and exotic Eastern music wafted through the house.

I called to Barb, and down the steps she came with every head scarf she owned pinned to a pair of purple tights, sheerness flying in all directions as her hips swayed left and right. The batting veil was provocatively arranged across her face, and things were jingling and jangling all over her body and—GOOD GRIEF—she was belly dancing!

If she hadn't given away the couch the previous

week, I would have sunk onto it. As it was, I made it into a straight-back chair and watched in fascination. She was pretty darned good, too. At one point as she executed a very interesting maneuver for a 60-year-old woman, I said, "What do you call that?"

"The snake," she replied.

Interesting.

Well into the dance now and giving it her best, she took a moment to inform me that belly dancing was the oldest continuous folkloric dance. By then I was well past looking for any educational value.

Salome was doing great right up until her bracelet bangles got hung in her veil, and then she started laughing and the dance was over.

"This was quilting I just saw, wasn't it?" I surmised.

"You got it," she said. "Were you surprised?"

"I don't think I've ever been more surprised," I told her.

She said Laura had thought she'd given it all away. "She left me messages everywhere that night, apologizing," Barb said. "But I told her, "Oh, Randy doesn't suspect. You could have told him anything.""

Husbands love to hear things like that.

The next time I saw Betts, I asked, "Why didn't you tell me your sister was taking belly dancing lessons?"

"GOOD GRIEF!" she exclaimed. "I thought she said ballet dancing."

So now I come back to the question I have for you, my friend, the one I need your best advice on here. This woman has been lying like a yellow dog to me and others for two months, sneaking around behind my back, pretending to garner skills for the time-honored domestic enterprise of quilting, and laughing all the while at my gullibility with her friends.

So what do you think? Should I get her the flowers or the candy?

BARB: *Rand has this amazing ability to write full columns about nothing. I think he was doing it even before Seinfeld mastered the art. Once he wrote a column about a fan falling from our bedroom window to the ground below. His headline was, "Fitzgerald Fan Falls to Untimely Death." Now who wouldn't read that? This one is about nasal strips. (Try not to get too excited.)*

Barb and the Night Visitor

When daughter Sarah came back home to live for a few months recently before heading out west for her assignment with AmeriCorps, she greeted us in the hall one morning shaking her head in amazement. "I don't see how you two get any sleep at all," she said, groggily. "You both snore like the Texas Chain Saw Massacre has come to town."

Barb and I are well aware that we snore and well aware that the problem gets worse as we get older. If we don't go to sleep at the same time nowadays, one of us is sure to lie awake listening wide-eyed to the jackhammer on the other side of the bed. Some nights one or the other of us will get up and wander down to son Kyle's now empty room at the other side of the house and close the door to get a few hours of quality sleep.

That's why I was so happy to come up with the perfect solution at Christmastime. Watching football again had reminded me of those little plastic strips that a number of

From the *Richmond Times-Dispatch*, January 29, 2003

players wear across their noses to help them breathe better. I suddenly remembered that those strips could also be used to reduce snoring, so I bought a box, wrapped it up, and added it to Barb's stocking.

It's amazing how ungrateful women are when you put something in their stocking to help them stop snoring.

"Why is this in my stocking and not yours?" she asked.

"Because I needed some more things to fill yours up," thinking fast.

We decided one night early in the New Year to give those little strips a trial run. It soon became apparent that either I had purchased the wrong size or one or both of us were direct descendants of Jimmy Durante. Neither of us could stretch them as far across the nose as pictured on the box.

"Why did you get small/medium?" Barb asked.

"Because you told me not to buy anything for you ever again in a large size," I reminded her.

We looked pretty funny, both of us, with these silly little plastic strips across our schnozzles. It was hard to get them securely stuck down on each side, especially since the small/medium stuck only across the bridge of the nose and not down to the nostrils as recommended. But we did the best we could and settled in to see if blissful sleep lay ahead.

About one o'clock in the morning, I awoke with a start as Barb sat straight up in bed and yelled, "Wha? Whoo?"

Then she began flailing wildly in the dark. I could see enough by moonlight to know there was no one else in the room, so I had to assume she was flailing at some personal demons, especially after she suddenly smacked herself in the face. The slap rang out so loudly that Lucy Dog, who is pretty much deaf now, ran to the bedroom door to get the heck out.

"What in the world is wrong with you, honey? I asked, struggling to find the light.

Barb

As I did, Barb started to laugh. She rolled back onto her pillows and laughed like a crazy woman. She laughed until she shook the bed. I was awfully glad at that moment that Sarah had moved on to AmeriCorps because heaven knows what conclusions she might have reached about the hysteria in our bedroom.

When I found the lamp switch and took a look at my bride, I saw that one side of her nasal strip had popped up and was bobbing around to the left of her now bright-red nose. The other side was still attached.

Barb, still laughing, explained. "I woke up and opened my eyes a little and in the dark of the moon I saw something huge flying around very close to my face. I swatted it, but I couldn't seem to judge the distance right, and then I realized it was on my nose so I smashed it."

Almost instantly she had realized that she had beaten her nasal strip to death, not to mention her nose, and that was when she cracked up. Now she was crying, half from laughing and half from the pain of busting herself in the face.

"Maybe we better throw these things away," I told her, after we both stopped laughing. "I'm not sure the end to snoring is worth this."

"Well," she said, "don't worry too much about that because the reason I woke up in the first place is that you were snoring like a freight train."

BARB: *We are always delighted that readers write in so often to share their own stories with us. Many of Randy's columns over the years simply contained stories from his readers, sharing their own experiences. Often one of his columns would trigger a memory of something similar in their lives. I remember that after the previous column appeared, a letter came in from a woman who opened her eyes in the middle of a night to see a seemingly disembodied hand on her pillow. She reached over, half asleep and terrified, and tried to knock it away, but no matter how hard she hit at it, it remained right there. Just as she started screaming, she realized it was her own right hand, fast asleep and not feeling a thing, because her head was resting on that arm and had cut off the circulation. You truly can't make these things up.*

Barb's World-Famous Delicious Dumplings

Sunday afternoon brought something of a crisis to our house, one that involved chicken and flour, phone calls, dumplings and, it must be said, at best a serious deviation from truth and at worst a flat-out lie.

It all started when our son, Kyle, and I returned home around dark from playing golf to find Barb in a stew. Actually, the chicken was in a stew and ready to come out, but Barb couldn't find her dumpling recipe, the family recipe she's been using for 35 years.

"You mean you can't remember how to make the

From the *Richmond Times-Dispatch*, February 4, 1998

same dumplings you've been making for three and a half decades?" I questioned.

"Look, you can never remember where you put your shoes, and you've been wearing them for half a century," she pleasantly responded.

Trying to be helpful, I went to her recipe box and started pulling out index cards, hoping to find one that said, "BARB'S WORLD-FAMOUS DELICIOUS DUMP-LINGS," but before I got very far, she said, "No use looking in there."

So where would the recipe be if not in the recipe box, I queried.

My dear wife stood and drummed her fingers on the table for a few minutes before answering. She looked over at the roiling chicken. She looked at the ceiling. "Actually," she finally mumbled, "it's on the Bisquick box."

Dear reader, I don't mind telling you that I had to go sit down. "BARB'S WORLD-FAMOUS DELICIOUS DUMPLINGS," the soft and fluffy dumpling that I have been raving about for my entire marriage, are simply Bisquick?

"Well," Barb confessed, "they are. But I do add some extra ingredients that make them uniquely my own"

"And those extra ingredients would be . . .?" I asked. She paused again before saying, "Milk."

"Milk?"

"Milk."

Now I recognize that there are levels of deceit, some more serious than others, and in the great scheme of things, her passing off Bisquick dumplings as her own homemade recipe for all these years is a minor matter. But I must admit I was shaken. Was BARB'S THICK AND SPICY BRUNS-WICK STEW really a can of Mrs. Fearnow's? Come to think of it, why had we not once had BARB'S AUTHENTIC ITALIAN SPAGHETTI since the day the Venice restaurant closed down?

"You've always told me," I pouted, "that these dumplings were made with your own dear mother's recipe."

"They were," she assured me. "Mama used Bisquick, too."

Shaking my head and eyeing the stewing chicken, now spinning wildly like a gyroscope in its juices, I asked the obvious question. "If you've gotten the recipe off the box for all these years, why don't you just get it off the box tonight?"

"Because I bought the small box by mistake," she wailed, "and apparently the dumpling recipe is just on the large. Would you mind calling a few of the neighbors for me while I fix the salad," she pleaded, "and see if anyone has a large box of Bisquick on hand. Stick with Southern neighbors, Baptist neighbors or large-sized neighbors who probably eat a lot of dumplings."

No one I called had Bisquick. The chicken by now was starting to make little squeaking noises that sounded somewhat like desperate attempts at communication.

"I've got it," Barb suddenly exclaimed. "Call my sister and ask her."

Betts' husband answered the phone. "Clarence," I said, "we have something of an emergency here. Barb's lost the family dumpling recipe. Can we get it from Betty?"

I heard him yell to his wife. "Betty," he said, "will you come to the phone and give Randy your recipe for BETTY'S WORLD-FAMOUS DELICIOUS DUMPLINGS?"

No Granny Panties, Please

For my wife Barb's 70th birthday this summer, a group of young people she worked with in the early 2000s threw her a surprise birthday party. They've stayed in touch with her over the years, continuing to invite her to lunches and happy hours, Yankee swaps at Christmas and shopping trips to Williamsburg.

All of them may finally be somewhere in their 30s now, but when Barb was their colleague, most of them were 20-somethings, a few fresh out of college, whereas Barb was about 60 at the time.

She adored every one of them. They invigorated and challenged her, and I think she kept them amused. She told me back then that we should never move into a retirement home where all the people would be older. "Different ages have gifts to offer each other," she said. "These girls take me back to a wonderful time in my life, and I show them they'll still be wild and crazy in their 60s."

Barb drove a carload of them to lunch one day. She has a bit of a heavy foot, and as she was driving along at her usual lively pace, darting in and out of traffic a bit, Susan said, "I'm surprised that you drive so fast."

And Barb replied, "Well, I try not to drive like an old woman."

At that Gabe chimed in from the back seat: "Well, then, maybe you'd better turn off your turn signal."

At the recent surprise party, Laura and Lynnie had

From *Boomer* magazine, October-November 2011

baked cakes, Paige got it organized and everyone kicked in on a present—and the present for a septuagenarian was as much a surprise as the party. It was a $125 gift certificate to an adult lingerie shop! Barb described it to me as a place that sold "frillies, flimsies and funsies," including games and gadgets—and then she invited me to go along on her shopping trip.

It was an interesting place, owned by a nice lady and frequented by seemingly upscale kinds of women, most of whom were less than middle-aged. Barb went directly to the lingerie while I paused briefly at garter belts. They were interesting. Men of a certain age seem often to have a kind of fascination with garter belts. Garter belts are something we men were curious about in our youth, and they remain interesting. I feel sure Lauren Bacall wore a garter belt. Pantyhose do not have the same charm.

The store did have some items for men. I saw massage oils, books and playful items for both sexes—including a game called Randy Raffle. Interesting.

While Barb tried on silky, satiny, lacy, filmy nightgowns, I tore myself away from the garter belts and eased into a corner between the fur handcuffs and the underwire bras and made myself small, which is not a real challenge for a 5'6" man.

Of course, when you're in an adult lingerie store with ladies holding up interesting underwear for inspections, it's hard to feel unobtrusive. No granny panties here, folks.

I must confess I made a small purchase myself. I don't want to say what it was because I would like to continue to keep this column for a while. But when Barb and I saw it, we both said at once, "We have to buy that for Terry."

Terry is my brother. I won't say what we bought for him, but I will say that he found it interesting.

While a Guitarist Not-so-Gently Weeps

"**O**h, my Lord, she's backed over my guitar."
That was my first thought when I heard the clunk and felt the thump from my passenger seat as Barb backed us out of the driveway at the beginning of a recent week-long getaway.

That was my first thought, but my first word after that thump is best left to the wind.

Every guitar-playing fellow or lady out there reading this will understand immediately my horror at the sound and feel of the back tires rolling onto something formidable just at the moment you suddenly remember leaving the guitar case propped against the trunk.

Last year, after all the damage to the Gulf Coast from Hurricane Katrina, I wrote that there were only a very few possessions it would break my heart to lose. One of them was the Martin guitar Barb and the kids gave me for Christmas in 1997.

Now that very guitar might really be lost. I had left it behind the car because Barb has her own organized system for packing the car for trips and likes to load everything herself. Though I had mentioned to her that it was back there, both of us then promptly forgot that it was.

I thought back to that magical Christmas when all I had received had been ties and socks, socks and ties, present after present of just those while the rest of the family opened the wonderful treasures I had chosen for them.

From *Richmond Times-Dispatch*, May 5, 2006

Finally, the last present opened, Barb said, "Well, I guess that's it." And I sat there kind of dumbfounded, surrounded by socks and ties, as the family headed off to the kitchen for breakfast. At the door, that coy little threesome suddenly turned and Barb said, "Oh, wait, I think we forgot one."

And off the sun porch came a badly wrapped present of an unmistakable shape. I knew immediately it was a guitar, but when I saw that it was a Martin, I could have wept.

That Martin guitar has been with me every day since—mostly in my hands, always in my soul. Sitting in the car that day, afraid to get out and look, my musical life flashed before my eyes.

I remembered the time I thought I might join a jam session in the parking lot in Galax at the Old Fiddlers Convention and, attempting to swing the guitar smoothly from my back to my front, I dropped it resoundingly on the ground.

I remembered the thrill of my stage "debut" last year at the Chickenstock Festival in Montpelier.

I remembered so many Jahnke Road Tuesday night sessions and jamming with friends on the porch at The Cabin on the Ridge in Mouth of Wilson, Virginia.

I thought about all the pickin' and grinnin' that got done on annual beach trips with Cousin Dick Morris and my nephew Steve Walker.

These are the kinds of memories guitar players cherish, of new friends made, fellow pickers they've bonded with, and funny things that happen.

A guitar is more than a hobby. If you love it, it's like an appendage. I hope all of you have something, a "thing" in your life that you can love as much as I love my guitar.

So, with Barb saying, "Oh no, oh no, oh no," I walked warily to the rear of the car.

The case had not fared well. My black "CASH" decal was shredded and the "Dr. Ralph Stanley for President" sticker in tatters.

One lock was completely broken, another badly bent but, amazingly, the case had held firm. The car had passed over or against the neck end of the case, but the guitar inside was—hard to believe—undamaged.

The folks at Guitar Works tell me that saving the case is beyond them—it would need to go to a luggage repair place.

"Actually," Barb said, "with all the scrapes and scars and the locks beat up like this, it has a lot of character. It suits you better now."

I do hope she wasn't thinking of that country song, "I Ain't Broke, but I'm Badly Bent."

Randy

BARB: *Randy kids me all the time about being a ditz, but he's not exactly a Type A personality himself. He chose each of the columns in Chapter Five himself, trying, he said, "to create an honest image of the kind of fellow I am." (I'm the one who decided to put the ditzy one first.)*

Losing a Truck Puts Misplacing Glasses in Focus

People who don't know any better always tell me how much they envy my laid-back personality. What they see is an easygoing, happy-go-lucky sort who never seems to get

From *The Richmond News Leader*, July 5-6, 1989

CACKIE TRIPPE MCCARTY
The Pepsi truck was not stolen, but maybe the Pepsi shirt was.
(Randy wants you to notice that it still fits today, 40 years later.)

67

frazzled or stressed.

What they don't see is a man whose life is constantly punctuated with frantic, last-minute searches for keys and glasses, reports and briefcases, wallets and shoes. Unless you're one of my brethren, you can't possibly grasp the trauma of never knowing where things are. The thought that mine may not be the ideal personality type came home to me the summer I lost the Pepsi Cola truck, but I'll get to that in a moment.

My poor wife, Barbara, learned 30 years ago never to give me a watch or a ring. I must have lost a half-dozen of the latter, including three gold wedding bands and both her and my high school rings.

When it comes to pens or keys, I'm even more hopeless. Be it a Bic or a Montblanc, it has a 30-minute lifespan in my hands. The few keys I haven't lost in my life have remained with me simply because I probably locked them in my car, usually in the ignition with the motor running.

My dad used to tell of the time he invited me to play golf with him in Waynesboro. He even let me drive his new car the 25 miles over the mountain from Charlottesville to get there. At the end of the match and near the end of the day, I discovered I had lost the keys somewhere on the course. We had to call a cab to drive us home. (This is one of those stories that are a lot funnier today than at the time.)

Books are another problem. After meaning to read "Ragtime" for a number of years, I finally took along a copy on vacation last year. During one of our stops, I set it temporarily on the roof of the car while I searched for keys, then drove away with it there. The first half of the book, I can tell you, was excellent.

Losing "Ragtime" was a mere inconvenience. But some losses are much more serious. I have lost so many pairs of glasses in the last 10 years that I'm on a first-name basis with Mary at the optical company. You might recall a column a couple years back about my sitting down on my glasses in the rush to get to son Kyle's T-ball game. Since Mary swiftly prepared a new pair for me, I was able to enjoy seeing the world again for about two weeks.

But, alas, one day Clarence, my brother-in-law, had the audacity to run over the new pair with his riding lawn mower. I had laid them carefully on his lawn not four hours previous to his blundering carelessness, but by the time I missed them, he had already thoughtlessly wiped them out in a swoop.

You'd be amazed at the damage a riding mower will do to a pair of glasses. Mary certainly was. "If you had any lens left," she said, "they'd still be under warranty. But slivers don't count." Thanks a lot, Clarence.

I've lost so many glasses, electric razors on trips, and umbrellas that I automatically get all three from family members each Christmas. I understand their certainty that I am always in need of replacements for those things, and I even share their lack of confidence in me, ever since I lost the Pepsi truck.

The second week after turning in my grades at VSU and beginning my summer job as a Pepsi delivery man, I drove my Pepsi truck to a huge grocery warehouse, unloaded numerous cases of drinks and wandered through the cavernous innards of the building to get the proper forms signed.

When I went back out onto the loading dock, my truck had disappeared. The warehouse manager was called in. Police were notified. My boss at Pepsi was called and showed up at Loading Dock A, where crowds were gathering. About the time the big boss arrived, a fellow who worked on the other side of the building walked up and said to me, "Uh, would you mind coming over to Loading Dock B and moving your truck? It's been blocking access for an hour."

I mean, gee whiz, if a man can lose a Pepsi truck, what chance do these little eyeglasses have? See you soon, Mary. Give my best to your husband, Pete.

Pampered Chef Party

*L*ast Friday evening I was privileged to boldly go where no man has gone before.

I was the lone male among some 40 females in attendance at a Pampered Chef party in what is probably on most nights the quiet suburban neighborhood of Crestwood Farms in Chesterfield County. On this night, it was anything but quiet.

Barb has been going to Pampered Chef parties for some time now, coming home full of smiles and gossip, raving about the great food and drink she has just enjoyed. So when her good friend Stephanie (who is a great cook, not to mention partial to snakeskin pants) was hostess at a P.C. party last weekend, I wrangled an invitation so I could educate us males about what actually goes on at these mysterious gatherings.

Sit back, fellows, and I'll give you the lowdown. When you are home alone on a Friday night, reclining on your couch innocently watching "Law and Order" and picturing your wife at the modern-day equivalent of a quilting bee, let me enlighten you.

She is drinking wine. A lot of wine. She is eating better than you have since you last invested an entire paycheck at a top-notch restaurant. She is tallying up purchases that may well reach triple figures before the evening ends. And she is talking out loud to women friends about YOU.

I got some strange looks when I walked in, believe me, until our lovely Pampered Chef representative for the

Fro the *Richmond Times-Dispatch*, March 1, 2000

Randy

DOUGLAS PAYNE

evening told the other guests I was there to write a column; after that, I was just one of the girls.

The party quickly divided into two contingents. There was the noisy partying element in the kitchen who already knew what they'd be buying, and the polite sit-down group in the living room. Most of us in the living room were the novices, listening to the Pampered Chef spiel and watching various kitchen products demonstrated as treats like roasted chicken pizza with onion and rosemary were being prepared for the waiting ovens.

Scrambled eggs being the extent of my cooking expertise, I had expected to be bored, but the products were interesting. There were man-sized hot mitts displayed, which I immediately put down on the order form handed to me upon arrival. I also like the sturdy look of the stoneware and ordered several pieces of that. I had just signed up for the ice cream dipper and the tomato corer when Barb showed up from the kitchen and took away my order form.

71

I headed out sheepishly with her to join the fun in the kitchen. Our hostess kept introducing me to lovely ladies and they all kept hugging me, which was nice. Stephanie explained that women always hug when they meet in social situations like this. "Even someone you might dislike?" I asked. "Oh, sure," she said. "You just hug the ones you like a little harder."

Jo Ann put some liquid refreshment in one of my hands and a big plate of tomato and basil foccacia bread and Grecian party squares in the other hand, while Barb held my wine and women kept hugging me. I decided this was one of the best parties I'd been to in a long time.

I was brought back to earth somewhat when an announcement was made that whoever had parked the van in the driveway had to move it because "the men have to get out."

For a minute I thought I was being asked to leave, but soon realized there were other men in another part of the house at that moment who were not participating in the party and were now for some reason ready and eager to leave.

I wondered if perhaps the word had filtered back to the den or the basement or wherever the husbands of the huggers had gathered that there was some guy in the kitchen with the women, drinking wine, eating hors d'oeuvres and purchasing lemon zesters. So they polished off their beers, put out their cigars, turned off ESPN and headed out to their Ram trucks.

"C'mon, Jud," says Paulie. "Let's get outta here before I have to straighten out dat pipsqueak in the kitchen wid the girls."

Once Jud and Paulie and the guys had left, all the women descended on the kitchen where magnificent dishes were coming out of the oven.

We eat. We drink. We hug. We buy. We talk politics and poetry, menus and menopause. Barb drives us home.

Jud and Paulie don't know what they missed.

72

Randy

RANDY: *It's a good thing our country neighbor Billy, who lived just down the lane from the farmhouse, never heard that I had attended a Pampered Chef party. He and many of the other good old boys who lived around there clearly thought I was about the most citified dolt they'd ever run across, so I tried not to eat quiche or sip tea around them. Billy was onto me, though. Here's an excerpt from a 2010 column "Wild Life."*

City Slicker

...One day there was a great thrashing about inside the rusty oil barrel we kept for burning our trash at the farm, but Barb and I were reluctant to stick our heads over the side to see what was trapped in there, or to turn it over and release the prisoner until we knew what it was. Might have been a skunk. Or a snake. So I walked down the lane a piece to Billy's house and asked him what we could do. He allowed as how he'd take care of it, and he came walking up the path a few minutes later with his rifle, walked fearlessly to the barrel, peered over, reached in and rustled some papers out of the way and said laconically, "Possum." And he raised his gun.

"No, no," I yelled. "Don't shoot it. Don't shoot it."

That evening I arrived at the country store a mile up the road just in time to hear Billy regaling the farmers around the potbellied stove with a story they apparently found tremendously amusing. The punch line seemed to be, "Don't shoot it. Don't shoot it."

Excerpted from *Boomer* Magazine, April-May 2010

Batter Up

*L*et me say right off the bat that Barb is not going to find this column one bit funny. She has found very little to laugh about for days. It started . . .

MONDAY, 2 A.M.: I am awakened from a dream in which I have just stepped up to the plate at The Diamond, wearing a Braves uniform, when people start to scream "Bat! Bat!"

I am thinking "That's what I'm trying to do, folks," when suddenly I am wide awake as Barb comes like a bat out of hall, into bedroom, across her side of the bed and onto mine, with 11-year-old Sarah close on her heels. This time there is no mistaking the message: There is a bat in the house.

I don't know how you feel about bats, but the little furry flying fellows are not real high on the welcome list at my house. There was little sleep for the rest of that night.

MONDAY, LATER IN THE DAY: Barb makes a phone call to a pest control company, and the owner spends a lot of time reassuring her that our bat is totally harmless and that it's as frightened of her as she is of him. He points out that bats are beneficial, that they eat about 2,000 insects a day, and that only one half of one percent of them are rabid. He also says there is a good chance the bat has already retreated the same way he came in.

We want desperately to believe this, but the only part of the discussion that really sticks with Barb is his admission that, yes, bats sometimes do fly into one's hair—but usually only when the breeze is blowing the hair about. Once she

From the *Richmond Times-Dispatch*, September 2, 1992

heard that, Barb started wearing a baseball cap around the house.

That afternoon the pest people show up, wearing their own baseball caps, ones with a Batman emblem on them, ready to stage the First Great Bat Hunt. They rattle three bookcases full of kids' toys and games. They shake sheets in the linen closet. They look in shoes and potted plants. They check radiators and air conditioning vents. They do not find a bat.

TUESDAY: Here's where the story picks up. I have one of my rare trips out of town, so Barb and Sarah are home alone. (Son Kyle wisely chose this week to be off at the beach.)

Barb and Sarah hurry home with Chinese food well before dark, lock up the house, put on the alarm system and barricade themselves in the back of the house in our bedroom and my adjoining study, all lights blazing.

They even go so far as to push the dresser against the one door out, and then they settle down to egg rolls and fried rice, worrying not of man nor beast.

At exactly 9:30 as Barb reads in the study, sans baseball cap, and Sarah watches "Beverly Hills 90210" from my easy chair, the bat comes out of nowhere and begins to swoop and flap around the two rooms. They are now barricaded WITH the bat. And Barb's hair is definitely moving around, and moving fast.

After a scene best not described here, Barb and Sarah re-barricade themselves in the study, bat standing guard outside in the bedroom. At some point during the next long hour's siege, Barb picks up the fortune from Sarah's long-forgotten fortune cookie. "Your home," it says, "is a calm and pleasant place to be."

NEXT WEEK*: Barb and Sarah move to the Holiday Inn. Randy spends a night as the Caped Crusader. And the bat goes on.

---

* I.e., next page.

Gotham is Saved

*L*ast week we left my wife and daughter locked up in my study, hiding from a bat loose in the house. This was the point at which Barb called 1) the friendly bat man from last week's column, who wasn't home, 2) the Richmond police, who provided the number of another pest control company, 3) the other pest control company, who advised Barb to put on gloves and toss the bat out the window, 4) a neighbor with a spare key to unlock the front door, and 5) another neighbor, Charlie Rowland, who came over with his teenage son Darin and bravely staged The Second Great Bat Hunt in two days. No bat.

When the neighbors left, Barb and Sarah followed them out the door, on their way to the Holiday Inn. When I pulled up in front of my deserted home at 10 that night, every light was blazing. And through the front windows, I could see the bat, soaring and diving and having a grand old time.

Have I made clear that I do not fancy bats? Sitting there in the car watching that creature weave and bob past the windows, I remembered the piece of advice Barb had given me when I called the Holiday Inn earlier to say I would handle the bat. "If you happen to go up into the attic and find a coffin, get out of the house immediately."

I remembered, too, my introduction to bats. About 20 years ago, I was sitting in the press box at Fluvanna High School covering a boring 400-to-zip football game when I spied a swarm of something crossing the playing field from the opposite bleachers.

From the *Richmond Times-Dispatch*, September 9, 1992

Randy

At first I thought my bleary eyes were playing tricks, but as the black cloud got closer, my lips silently formed the word "bats." They never slowed down. When they hit the open press box, it was every man for himself. I thrust my clipboard up in front of my face and one hit it—Whap!—and bounced off.

All around me reporters were scrambling around and saying things like "Gosh darn it" and "Gee whiz." This night is not one of my more pleasant life memories.

And neither was the one I was about to face. But a man's gotta do what a man's gotta do. So I headed into the house, put on my raincoat and baseball cap and got a tennis racket in hand. When I got to the bottom of the stairs and looked up, he was waiting for me on the top step, sitting there looking back at me, and we were just about at eye level.

I could read his thoughts, and he was saying, "You and I are going to rock and roll tonight."

And I said back to him, out loud, "I'm ready for you, dude."

Two and a half hours later, I finally got him under a bucket and took him outside to the night sky. During that time, I had chased him all over the house. I had opened every window in the place. Again and again I tried to brush him off curtains, beds, walls. I dodged, he circled. And gradually as the night got to be morning, I lost my fear of him.

The pest control man had said that sometimes bats will shriek at you if you corner them. "But don't be afraid," he said, "because what they are really saying is, 'Oh, please don't hurt me.'"

I heard my bat say that near the end of our marathon encounter, and I found myself talking to him, again out loud, this time soothingly. "I won't hurt you," I said. "Everything's going to be all right."

And it was. On one of his swoops, I tried to guide him toward a window with the broom. Instead, he struck the broom and crashed to the floor, and I had my bucket ready.

When I uncovered the bucket
in the alley, he crawled to its edge, paused
a moment and took off in a perfect flight
pattern under the moon.

The best moment came early the next
morning when I could call Barb and Sarah
and tell them they had a home again. They
were ecstatic, and I wouldn't have been a
bigger hero had I saved all of Gotham.

DOUGLAS PAYNE

A Polka-Dot Kind of Guy

Joe Seipel's polka-dot bow tie and cummerbund were big hits at a downtown hotel last weekend.

Too bad Joe couldn't have been there to get all the compliments.

I myself was the beneficiary of Joe's good taste, though if you could have seen me an hour earlier madly throwing clothes out of dresser drawers at home and emptying closet shelves as I looked for my own tux accessories, you would have indentified me as a centerfold for Psychology Today rather than GQ.

I have this bad habit of waiting until the last minute to throw my ensemble together when Barb and I are going out. Invariably I'm ironing the right shirt at the last minute or chasing down socks that match.

"Can I get away with wearing these brown shoes?" I yell in to Barb when my shiny blacks don't turn up under any of the beds.

"Only if you're planning to go with Rosanne Barr," she yells back.

When the children still were living at home, sometimes they'd just pull up a chair and watch me get ready for an evening out, and if a tuxedo was involved, they sometimes would pop popcorn and take pictures as well.

It's a show, all right.

Last Saturday evening I had to be in place, downtown, at 6 o'clock sharp, tuxedoed and slicked back, for an initiation ceremony.

At 25 minutes to 6, I still was at our home in greater Ginter Park, expanding my colorful vocabulary in periodic outbursts from the depths of hatboxes and old suitcases, looking for anything appropriate to wear around my neck.

My ruffled shirt was crispy clean, my tux pants were maintaining their crease as I crawled around the closet floor, my shoes were spit-polished, my studs were in place, but my bow tie was missing.

Barb got on the phone calling neighbors to see who might provide a replacement for the evening. (It was unclear whether she meant a replacement for me as her escort or a replacement for the bow tie.) It quickly became apparent that all the guys on our block, except me, apparently had donned their tuxes that night and gone out together for a meeting of the Mystic Knights of the Sea. In any case, there was neither a male nor a bow tie to be found.

Moving on to the next block, Barb found a tie immediately.

"Ha!" she said in triumph. "I figured a dean would have one."

And right she was. Joe Seipel, an associate dean at VCU and formerly head of the sculpture department, did indeed own a tux, so we stopped off at his and Suzanne's house for the bow tie on our way downtown.

What I had not considered was this: Not only is Joe Seipel a dean, but he is—even more so—an artist. So when Barb returned to the car with a black and white polka-dot bow tie and matching cummerbund, I was a little taken aback.

As grateful as I was for the loan, I've never considered myself a polka-dot kind of guy.

"Put it on and be quiet," Barb said, sympathetically.

When we arrived at the hotel, the very first fellow I ran into said, "Hey, Randy, I like that tie." And when I stepped off the elevator, a lady I didn't even know said, "Great bow tie there."

Randy

All night, amid a sea of tuxes in the meeting room, the compliments kept coming. "Looking spiffy, brother" and—cruel truth—"Somebody must have given you that tie because you're not that cool."

The polka-dot bow tie now is back with its rightful owner, but I still haven't found the solid black one that I usually wear with my tux. But while I don't know exactly where it is, I do know now how it got away from me.

The other day Barb produced from daughter Sarah's room a snapshot from Christmas 2002. In it Moe, our tuxedo cat, is sitting proudly under the tree, his white vest clean and resplendent in the bright flash of the camera. He is wearing, I notice, a bow tie.

CHAPTER SIX

Uncle Roy

BARB: *Uncle Roy appeared in more columns than anyone except Rand, me and the kids. He was my old bachelor uncle who lived in a white frame farmhouse "across the path" from the smaller farmhouse where I grew up. Randy and I inherited that house when my daddy, Roy's older brother, died in 1984. It gave us great weekend proximity to Uncle Roy, his country ways and his country humor.*

Uncle Roy had a wicked sense of humor, loved to play tricks on people, enjoyed a cold beer, had an excessively colorful vocabulary, was tight as a tick and, sometimes, mean as a snake. You never knew which Roy you'd get when you visited. After one trip to his house when the kids were small, on a day when we found him snappish and critical, little Sarah asked on the way home, "Mom, tell me again. What is it we like about Uncle Roy?"

The four columns we've chosen chronicle not a

Uncle Roy sadly contemplates his empty beer cup.

83

man's life but a journey to death. We chose them, rather than some of his light-hearted adventures, because they form a tribute to his indomitable spirit and his love of life. They help to explain, too, what it is that we liked about Uncle Roy.

DEATH
IN THE FAMILY
THE UNCLE ROY STORIES

A Christmas Miracle

Christmas is the time of year when everything is exaggerated. Expectations are at their highest, depression at its worst, joy is intense and so is grief. Around our house, we've had a fair share of both this season.

Our lowest moment came, as it does in so many homes, with the 5 a.m. phone call that announces trouble—in our case, the serious illness of Barb's 79-year-old Uncle Roy in Charlottesville. A lot of families have a relative like Uncle Roy. He's the one you think will live forever.

But this time, a week before Christmas, the prognosis was bad. The doctors said it was pneumonia and bronchial problems, aggravated by severe lung damage for 65 years of smoking. Within days, Roy was often unable to breathe and often delirious.

Barb and her two sisters, Betty and Ruby—his only relatives left—rallied round, taking shifts of sitting with their

From *The Richmond News Leader,* January 1-2, 1992

uncle, spoon-feeding him, interpreting his weak voice for the doctors and nurses.

Barb regularly drove back and forth between our house and the University of Virginia Medical Center, trying to balance the Christmas demands here with her need to somehow drag the old gentleman who has been such a constant in her life back from the edge of death.

On the two nights his sitters didn't show up, Barb stayed at his bedside herself, replacing his oxygen tube when he pulled it out, ringing for help when he had one of his spells.

Christmas shopping and decorating were put aside at three households as the family crisis took over.

When the kids' school held its annual Christmas program, for the first year the Fitzgeralds were not there. In Charlottesville, Betty canceled her much-anticipated Christmas trip to Disney World, and Ruby showed up at the hospital at dawn to get some juice down her uncle before she went to work.

Through it all, Roy wandered in and out of lucidity. "How's Mama this morning?" he asked Barb one night, referring to his mother who died in 1950.

"I was able to answer him honestly," she told me later. "I just said, 'She's the same.'"

Another time, Uncle Roy, a dedicated life-long bachelor, was asked by a young doctor why he had never married. After long hours of delusion, Roy very clearly replied, "Because I always thought I'd rather go through life wanting something I didn't have than having something I didn't want."

One day, the doctors feared that Roy might have a blood clot in a lung, so they took him downstairs for some lengthy tests. One was very difficult for him. They took away his oxygen and asked him to breathe into a hose that contained some radioactive particles that would trace through his lungs.

He was already gasping for breath, and it was all he could do to follow their instructions. Just when Barb thought he'd gotten through it, the doctors decreed that he had to do it all over again.

Finally, exhausted and pale, he was wheeled out into the hall to await the orderly who would take him back to his room. As Barb stood over him, he murmured something, and she bent close to hear him whisper, "Tough old buzzard." Only he didn't say "buzzard."

On Christmas Eve, the doctors began to talk life support. The drugs weren't working, the spells were more frequent, he was weakening away. "If we put him on a respirator for a while," they said, "and gave his lungs a chance to rest, he might come back."

Barb and her sister agonized over the decision. They knew that if anyone was a fighter, a "tough old buzzard," their uncle was. But they also knew he had a living will and did not want to be hooked up to machines.

Ultimately, because they alone knew Uncle Roy's spunk, they told the doctors to go ahead with the respirator, but it was not needed.

Late that night, Uncle Roy came back. The congestion loosened, and he became lucid. By Christmas Day, he was sitting up, asking for a banana. It was like something out of "The Waltons."

When the doctor came in and told him he was on his way to recovery, Roy said, "I would never have made it without Brother's girls. All the family I've got is these three nieces, and they've been gifts from heaven."

For the "girls," all in their 50s now, Uncle Roy's comeback has been the greatest of Christmas presents.

And Christmas of '91, instead of being marked forever as the one at which we lost Uncle Roy, will be celebrated instead as the one at which we all started to believe in miracles.

Uncle Roy

Home from the Dead

Uncle Roy died for a little while last month, but if you could have seen him Sunday on his lawn tractor, you never would have believed it.

I last wrote about Roy, our old bachelor uncle, five years ago, the first time he was hospitalized and nearly died before making a miraculous recovery on Christmas Eve. I don't know why that comeback was such a surprise to us because Roy has always been full of miracles.

Now, at 83, he's still pulling them off. The day before the heart attack that sent him to the hospital this time, he hooked up his bush hog and cut three fields on his farm near Charlottesville. He went down to the shed where he keeps his washing machine and ran a load of overalls, and in the afternoon he got down on his knees and crawled under his Chevy to fix something there.

The next morning, he called Barb's sister to report that he might be dying. He was right. He was. The rescue squad no more than got him to the hospital than he stopped breathing. And because in the excitement no one had told the doctors he had a living will, he was resuscitated and put on a respirator.

Now he's back home, sitting out in a metal chair near his back door, catching a cool breeze, enjoying one more summer at the house where he was born and where he's lived his entire life. Sitting there with him means hearing the latest news from his little farming community, watching the white-tailed rabbit that's been occupying his yard all spring, laugh-

---

From the *Richmond Times-Dispatch*, June 19, 1996

ing at his jokes and comfortably passing time. All reason tells you he hasn't got a lot of that left.

He recalls nothing of his first few days at the hospital. But the rest of us remember how pitiful and unlike himself he was, tied to the bed, unable to communicate because of the tube down his throat but trying desperately to say something every minute we were there. "What are we putting him through?" his three devoted nieces kept asking. "This is exactly what he didn't want."

When the tube was removed, he didn't know them. Barb spent an entire day sitting by his bed while he told her his life story, thinking she was a hospital employee. All he knew for certain was that he wanted to go home, and even at 83, after a heart attack, no one could handle him. Despite his restraints, one day he managed to get a foot on the floor and slide himself, bed and all, across the room to the door.

Now at home again, he is himself, and content. Content to sit on his sun porch and read the paper. Content with a big class of buttermilk. Delighted with every phone call. Life is simple. Life is good.

Always fiercely independent, he now gratefully accepts the dumplings and pork roasts and banana pudding that find their way to his door. He's happy for others to organize the dozen pills he takes every day so he won't confuse them. He's appreciative when a niece delivers his paper from the highway box each morning, glad to read the obituaries and not find his name.

So the family ponders: When the next attack comes, what do we do then?

Had we been at the hospital the morning of his attack, living will in hand, he would not have had this summer, this June—the 84th June of his life.

Does one more June matter? One more flock of honking geese flying overhead, forcing your eyes to the blue sky? One more summer's caress of warm sun on your face? One more cool June breeze drifting in the window at night?

One more cold watermelon under a shade tree? One more baseball game on the radio? One more chorus of children's laughter, ringing up from the house in the bottom? One more whippoorwill? One last apple dumpling, made of apples from the tree you planted, visible from your front window?

His second night home, Roy decided to get up in the middle of the night and walk through his home. The nurse staying with him was helping him along when suddenly he lost his balance and fell, unhurt, to the floor, with the nurse, a rather large woman, landing right on top of him.

"Lord, Mr. Roy," she told him. "Let me get up from here before I crush you."

As Rosa recounted his response later, she shook with laughter: "Take your time, Rosa. I'm 83 years old, and this may be my last chance to enjoy a moment like this."

What's it worth—one last chance at a hug and a joke?

From where I sit, waving to Uncle Roy in his doorway as my family pulls away after a visit, one more summer, one more June, one more hug, are worth just about anything. I'm glad we all have one more chance at them.

'We've Lost Uncle Roy'

When we got home from the funeral, we took the Christmas present we'd bought him out from under the tree and wondered what to do with it now.

It was the kind of gadget old men love, something he'd seen advertised in the slick, colored insert section of his

From the *Richmond Times-Dispatch*, December 11, 1996

Sunday paper. If you hook it up to your television, the ad claimed, all the wiring in your house becomes one big TV antenna and you suddenly get a dozen channels very clearly. Since he lived out in the country with no cable and not much in the way of reception, he was intrigued. So he saved the ad, and Barb secretly removed it from his desk drawer a month ago and ordered the thing for him for Christmas.

"I wish I'd gone on and given it to him at Thanksgiving," she said Sunday, turning the brightly wrapped Christmas package in her hand. "But how could we have known?"

How indeed. It's one of life's blessings that we can't.

Last Wednesday night my family went happily to sleep in Richmond and Uncle Roy went peacefully to sleep 60 miles up the road in his little farmhouse at Keswick, and none of us knew he'd never make it through the night. Even when someone has as much wrong as he did, even when they're just one month shy of 84, even when they've been near death many times, its actual arrival is still a broadside.

His death was about as good as it gets, though. He died in his bedroom in the house where he was born and lived his whole life. He couldn't have suffered more than a few minutes and probably wasn't even afraid when he had that last difficulty breathing—he'd had so many similar spells before.

Some nights his breathing got bad enough for him to hook himself to the oxygen next to his bed, sometimes bad enough to call in the middle of the night for the niece who lived next door and ask for help. Once every couple of months, the rescue squad got called, and maybe every other time he'd end up in the hospital. On one of those calls back in April, he'd stopped breathing and was brought back.

So he didn't sound alarmed when he called his niece just after midnight on Thursday. He simply said, as always, "I need some help." And she replied as always, "He's on his way." Roy was gone by the time help arrived.

He told Barb and me over Thanksgiving that when-

90

ever he called his niece at night like that, the longest it ever took her husband to roll out of bed, get dressed, cross the field and appear at his bedside was six minutes—"and he's usually faster than that."

We had shaken our heads at the image of the old man gasping for breath but still timing his nephew's arrival. That was Roy. He had to know the gas mileage his car was getting, the exact inches of rainfall yesterday and the number of people at everybody's funeral.

He would have been pleased at the turnout for his own. There were good friends of all ages, neighbors, former neighbors, the daughter of a once-but-long-deceased girl-friend, the village storekeeper, his favorite nurse, and a nice contingent of old railroad men who stood around in a circle, exchanging funny stories of their experiences when they and Roy all worked for the C&O.

I've told some of those stories in my columns, and I know a lot of people of my generation have the same kind of colorful, humorous, independent-minded bachelor uncles in their families, too. Quite often, these old gentlemen had cut a dashing figure with the ladies in their youth, as Uncle Roy had, but as their siblings married off and had their own families, a particular son—often the youngest—got left be-hind to take care of Mama. Of course, if Mama lived any length of time, life could pass the caregiver by, leaving him or her to become the bachelor uncle or the maiden aunt so familiar in family history.

I don't know where these self-sacrificing souls are among later generations. Maybe in the era of nursing homes, grown-up children don't feel the need to put their own lives on hold to look after aging parents. Uncle Roy, though, took a lot of pride in having done right by "Mama" and never seemed to regret the solitary life he led.

In the last few years, Uncle Roy's pleasures and needs were simple: an iron skillet full of corn bread, a visit or call from a friend, a flock of geese overhead, the petunias growing in the spare tire in the yard, and a chance to die in his own bed. Though it hurt to get the call—"We've lost Uncle Roy"—I'm glad he got his wish.

Stopping to Mourn

"I miss Uncle Roy," a woman said to Barb and me after our lunchtime speech at Welborne United Methodist Church last week. "The columns about him were always my favorites. I hated it when he died."

I'm sure Uncle Roy would have been amazed that so many people felt like they knew him.

Of course, my theory always was that everybody has an Uncle Roy in their family—at least the lucky ones among us do. He is that eccentric old fellow with a constant stream of stories, who loves to make people laugh, enjoys the neighborhood gossip and takes pride in his eccentricities—a character in the best Southern tradition.

When they pass on, these old treasures leave a hole in the family you'd never expect. Their passing is more than the end of a man, more like the end of an era. They become so much a given in one's life that even months later, you can't believe they're really gone. Sometimes we get little clues that Uncle Roy isn't.

Once during the days right after his death, when his three nieces were cleaning out his house, they were sitting in his living room sharing memories of him when suddenly a string on his guitar, leaning against a far wall, plunked as loudly as though some invisible hand had strummed it.

From the *Richmond Times-Dispatch*, September 24, 1997

Uncle Roy

Another time when they stood in his bedroom laughing about how much the old fellow had loved a dollar, the overhead light started to flicker on and off madly for a good 30 seconds.

And when they put a price tag on his big wood-framed mirror in preparation for the estate sale, the darn tag kept disappearing—three times that happened, with no one else in the house.

Of course, we want to believe he's around somewhere. How could that indomitable spirit be stilled?

He continues to color our lives. I'll never be able to eat squash without thinking of the summer he got down on his hands and knees to show me how to make a little hill and poke the squash seeds into it—two for me and one for the birds. I'll never be able to look over at the adjacent farm without seeing him in my mind's eye, striding across the path from his farmhouse to ours, to welcome us and to sit on the front porch and talk.

I'll never hear one of those mildly racy jokes he loved without wishing I could tell him the latest one I heard, and see him double over and slap his knee once more.

When I came across this poem recently, written by Michael Santa Barbara, a West Virginia lawyer who graduated from the University of Richmond in 1983, it was so real and true that I had to pause for breath. Change the word "grandfather" to "uncle," and it's Roy. Reprinted here with permission, it's called "Reflections after the Estate Sale."

I have not stopped to mourn
before now, but this morning,
old man, I found your tools,
mallets, files, open end wrenches
and knew finally that your
fierce, blue veined hands were quiet
and forgetful of a hammer's heft.

I went today, unafraid
to your work room and
found it empty and clean and impotent.
Gone were the malignant shadows and
bespectacled scowls that warned me,
as a child, away from your tools.

Seeing this place of yours readied for strangers, I
*   suspect that you are gone.*
I will mourn now, for in your leave taking I have
*   found that you were a man, and died as men will; alone*
*   and infirm. I will take comfort, however; you took a*
*   lion's share of life, and in your yielding you left not so*
*   much a grandfather, as the memory of a man I can love.*

Thank you for missing Uncle Roy, too, dear lady at the
church. I've written what I thought was the last Roy column
about three times now. This may be it. But probably not.

CHAPTER SEVEN

The Rest of the Family

BARB: *Almost all of our relatives are characters. We don't know how it got into both our bloodlines, but it certainly suggests that perhaps your family is strange, too. The whole world, it becomes obvious, is weird—which therefore makes us all normal. (Ross Perot was right—we all have a crazy old aunt in the attic.)*

Thinking back to the reader who said we created destiny when we named our cat Muffin, perhaps we doomed our kin to be eccentrics with family names like Uncle Pinks, Uncle Love, Aunt Tee, Aunt Willie, Uncle Fud and a grandmother-in-law called "Pa."

The One About the Brother

My brother Terry, the accountant, always has been careful with his money. He shakes his head at my carelessness. When I get up from a chair, I may leave as much as $12 in change rolling under the cushions. When I step from the car, quarters and dimes drop to the ground and between the seats. I never take a suit to the cleaners without a few dollars left in the pockets.

Terry knows the value of money and, unlike me, takes care of it. The only time I can remember that he turned money away came on a childhood trip my family made to Memphis in the early 1950s. At that point there were no rest stops on the highway—just an occasional picnic table by the side of the road and sometimes a privy a-ways down the clearing. At one such stop, there was a traveler in great distress. He had dropped his car keys down the privy and asked my father if, for a little money, he could hold either my brother or me by the heels and dangle us over the privy opening while we retrieved his set of keys, visible on top of the heap below. My father was aghast, of course, but I think Terry actually considered it. On the way back to our car, he asked, "How much do you think he would have paid?"

That makes this event all the more surprising.

A couple of weeks ago my sister-in-law, Frances, parked her no-longer reliable '84 Chevy at home and went out and bought herself a well-deserved Maxima. Brother Terry soon got tired of edging around the Chevy in the driveway and started thinking about how the tires on an un-

From the *Richmond Times-Dispatch*, July 27, 1994

necessary third car can mysteriously change into blocks over night. The Chevy had to go, and he was already considering a wise investment for the profits.

The best possibility seemed to be a used car dealer who could fairly assess the Chevy's value, fix what was crucial and ensure that the next owner would be happy with the purchase. The car looked great and, so far as they knew, had no major problems. It was just a bit old.

So after a hard day at work, Terry set off one evening to drive it over to a used car place on West Broad. Frances and their daughter, Tiffany, were to meet him there to drive him home once the deal had been struck.

After an hour's wait, however, Frances and Tiffany started to worry that perhaps he had broken down on the way there; and after another half hour, they were sure of it.

As Frances swung out into traffic to go look for him, Terry appeared, exiting from a strange car driven by a man she had never seen before.

"I got rid of the Chevy," said my brother. "Just sign over the title." Frances did so, pleased that Terry had found a buyer even before getting to the dealership.

On the way home, contemplating baubles, she asked, "Did he give you a check or cash?"

Terry frowned. "No, Frances," he said. "I didn't say I sold it. I said I got rid of it."

It turned out that the car had indeed broken down, just after Terry turned off Interstate 64 onto the exit ramp for Parham Road.

Terry is not a man to sit by the side of the road graciously. He has irons in the fire, places to go. He hates to wait, hates not to be in control, and hates a car that breaks down on him.

He waited awhile thinking someone would stop to help, but no luck there. Then he set out on a 90-degree evening to walk to the nearest place he could find a telephone. By the time he got there, he was hot, exhausted and riled.

"If I could find somebody to give me a ride to Broad Street to meet my wife," he said to the man who opened the door to let him in a building to use the phone, "I'd give them that darn car right now."

"Deal," said the stranger.

Terry figured he had saved about 60 bucks in towing charges, plus a lot of grief, and he was actually quite pleased with himself, until the next day when I gleefully showed him the Blue Book value of the Chevy, which came in at about four bills.

"I should have known better than to let you out of my sight," Frances grumbled. "It's Mad Man Dapper Dan all over again." For those of you new to Richmond, there used to be a used car dealer by that name in town, with a big sign out front that said, "Mad Man Dapper Dan. Would give 'em away but his wife won't let him."

Frances quickly figured out her share of the Blue Book value of the Chevy and presented Terry a bill. She's no slouch in the money department, either.

Map Quest

"How hard can it be?" I asked Barb as she sat down at her computer and I at my laptop to find a place to hold our upcoming Cousins' Weekend.

We have the entirety of six East Coast states in which to find a bed and breakfast with eight rooms available for our agreed-upon weekend. Piece of cake.

We've been having these cousins' reunions for several

years now, six or eight couples meeting each spring at towns like Fredericksburg and Tappahannock, bringing together as many as possible of the adult cousins from Barb's side of the family for a little sightseeing, shopping, good food and a chance to reconnect. The rest of the year it's kind of a wave-as-you-pass extended family.

Cousins come from as far away as New Jersey, so every state from there to Virginia qualifies as a potential site.

Three days later, with most of the hours in each day spent in front of our computers, we were still looking.

Barb thought Chincoteague would be great—quiet, with little to distract us from the hours we planned to spend sitting and talking. She quickly found an inn that looked perfect and sent out a preliminary email to see what the cousins thought of the idea.

Not much, it turned out. One cousin fired back a response so fast that Barb barely got the cursor off the word "send."

"I don't do bridges and tunnels," the cousin wrote. "I have never in my life crossed the Chesapeake Bay Bridge Tunnel, and I wouldn't do it even for Cousins' Weekend. In fact, if Elvis came back to life and was waiting for me on the other side, I still wouldn't cross the Bay Bridge."

OK, so much for Chincoteague.

"How about a B&B off I-81 somewhere," I suggested. "Like up in the Winchester-Middleburg area? This one looks perfect—and look at the reviews from people who've stayed there."

Barb took a look. "This inn welcomes pets," she noted. "Remember the year we got fleas? All the favorable reviews here are from pet owners grateful to have found a hospitable place, and I'm happy for them, but. . . ." Then she pointed out a negative review from a non-pet owner who said his room had reeked of cat.

Onward to West Virginia.

Cousin Nancy suggested a place in the Mountain

MARVA NOVITZ
Cousins Judy and Devi, with Randy,
at a gingerbread-style B&B in Cape May, N.J.

The Rest of the Family

State that looked good—a lovely inn near Civil War sites, but the New Jersey contingent wrote back to plead, "Please don't make us go to West Virginia."

Someone from New Jersey concerned about going to West Virginia?

"Baltimore!" wrote Cousin Dick. "Inner Harbor. Let's look there—Judy thinks she knows just the place."

Now it was my turn to protest. "Er, suppose we end up in a less-than-safe section of town," I worried. "We don't really know the city, and remember 'The Wire'? We don't want to get shot."

Someone from Richmond worried about getting shot in Baltimore?

On to Pennsylvania Dutch country! "Too rural," said Cousin Devi. "Mike and I like little villages with antique shops on these weekends, and around Lancaster you're basically out in the country with nothing around but horses and buggies."

Tangier Island has little shops. Now that's a great idea, especially with a couple of great B&Bs there just waiting for us.

"That trip puts the 'lug' in luggage," said Cousin Marva. "How do we get enough luggage for a long weekend across the water on that boat? We've got hairdryers and C-pap machines and rollators and—heck, Randy, you travel with a defibrillator."

True, old people travel is even more complicated than traveling with babies and kids.

At about this point, Barb interrupted her search long enough to sing a song to me she had just written about inns and areas nixed so far. If you remember the tune to "Sentimental Journey," please feel free to sing along:

Gonna nix a trip to Pennsylvania;
Gonna pass on "Bird-in-Hand."
We say no to "Mountain Inn" and "Dolly's,"
And all of West Virginia's banned.

101

FLIGHTS OF FANCY

(Chorus)

> *Balt'mer, that's where we'll get shot at, Balt'mer.*
> *And Jersey is anathema to us Rebs;*
> *"Welcome Inn" is overtop a deli,*
> *And on Tangier, there's no cabs.*

It actually had 10 verses, but you get the idea.

So after three days, how was the quandary resolved? We arbitrarily asked Cousins Betty and Jim to pick, thus taking the onus off ourselves if things went bad.

They made a good choice, admittedly—somewhere we've always wanted to go. This year the Cousins' Weekend will be held in Cape May, New Jersey. So far, everyone seems happy at the prospect.

Of course, we haven't heard from the West Virginia cousins yet.

MARVA NOVITZ

Jim and Norm relax with Randy for Cousins' Weekend in Cape May.

It's Enough to Make You Blue

*B*arb's sister Rue had occasion recently to sign up for a bus trip to Potomac Mills, a large factory outlet mall in Northern Virginia. The other ladies on the bus were all from the same church, and Rue reports that she enjoyed a full day of shopping with them.

She was delighted with her purchases: two gorgeous summer-weight sweaters that had been $50 each, marked down to half price. The salesclerk had chatted pleasantly with her, too, going on at length about what good buys Rue had found.

Back on the bus, heading home down Interstate 95, the ladies took turns standing up and holding high their purchases for the other women to admire. Rue even walked up and down the center aisle, holding first one sweater and then the other up against her blouse, so everyone could get a good look.

In hindsight, she thinks maybe the responses to her parade were a bit restrained.

Once home, she spread the sweaters on the guest room bed while she tried them on.

When she pulled the first one over her head, something seemed to go "clunk, clunk" against her earrings. And when she glanced in the mirror to see what it was, she was horrified to see hanging from the bottom of the sweater front one of those long, hard plastic things that stores clamp to their merchandise to prevent shoplifting.

"I was mortified," she says. "What in the world had

From the *Richmond Times-Dispatch*, July 29, 1992

those other women from church thought when they saw that piece of plastic hanging there."

To make matters worse, this was not the kind of plastic tag that sets off an alarm when you leave the store. It was the kind with a warning that said it was filled with a little packet of blue dye that would explode all over creation (and your sweater) if you tried to remove it yourself.

"I was angry," she told me. "I wrapped that sweater up and wrote a nasty note telling the store to remove that darn tag and mail me my sweater back, and that the salesclerk should stop talking so much and pay attention to what she was doing."

When Rue's husband, Earl (a former law enforcement officer) came in, he told his wife not to worry. He'd be happy to take care of it for her the next day. Thinking he meant he'd mail the package for her, she was stunned to come home the next day and find the sweater hanging in her closet. The plastic tag was gone.

"How did you do that so quickly?" she asked.

"I shot it," Earl said.

After she had gone to work, he had taken her sweater out, put everything but the offending tag inside a plastic bag, taped it up and hung it from a tree. Then he got his gun and neatly blew a hole between the sweater and the part of the tag that appeared to hold the dye.

"And I bet there wasn't really any dye in there anyway, right?" I asked.

"Bright blue," Rue said. "About half a cup. It all drained down on the ground where he shot it."

Rue has now worn her sweater several times and reports it to be comfortable, beautiful and a great bargain.

"I wear it everywhere," she says. "I haven't worn it to church yet, though."

RANDY: *This is another of the stories that families retell around the holiday table—"Remember the time that. . . ." It's excerpted here from a longer column I wrote on another subject. Gracie and her personality change were a family mystery for almost two weeks, and Barb and I were there for the denouement.*

Here, Kitty, Kitty!

My sister, Linda, had been complaining that her sweet little gray indoor-outdoor cat was undergoing an identity crisis. She noticed it when Gracie, who usually darted into the house the moment anyone opened a door, suddenly started refusing to come in at all. Linda called her name, cajoled and offered food, and Gracie just sat on the walk and stared like she'd never seen my sister before in her life. On a number of occasions, Linda had to go out and pick her up to bring her in, whereupon the kitty often immediately ran under the couch.

Some days Gracie was warm and playful—the old Gracie—and others haughty and stand-offish. On the latter days, even the dog, peering around the corner of doorways, knew not to come around her. In fact, any time the cat was in the house, the dog, formerly Gracie's good friend, took to disappearing.

On 8 a.m., Gracie might turn her nose up at the breakfast offering and meow at the door to get out, and 15 minutes later she'd be back to eat everything in sight, includ-

From the *Richmond Times-Dispatch*, November 7, 2001

ing the dog food. Some days she was so picky that Linda had to hand-feed her special new treats purchased just for her.

"What on earth is going on with this cat?" Linda kept asking her husband, Joel. "All of a sudden she scratches me, she runs from me, and I have to drag her into the house."

DOUGLAS PAYNE

"Do cats undergo menopause?" Joel asked, dangerously.

Linda took her to the vet, who could find nothing wrong with her and decided she must have been traumatized by something, and Linda took her home.

Saturday, just before Barb and I arrived there for dinner, the puzzle was solved. Standing at her kitchen window, Linda saw her sweet little gray cat in the yard, stalking a bird. Heading to the door to save the robin, Linda caught sight from the corner of her eye of something stretched out on the living room sofa. It was Gracie.

'Caught in a Trap'

Barb's sister Betts, who lives near our little farm near Charlottesville, called a while back to say a groundhog had dug a big hole and was now living under our farmhouse—a threat since groundhogs can collapse an old home if they dig enough around the foundation.

So Barb tracked down our Have-a-Heart trap, looked online to see what groundhogs eat, loaded the trap with half an apple, green grapes and a good helping of cabbage and headed to Keswick.

Before she even got back home, Betts called to say the trap had worked.

"Wonderful," I said. "We caught the groundhog then?"

"No," said Betts. "You caught a skunk."

Uh-oh.

How does one get a skunk out of a cage? The obvious answer is, very carefully. But in this case Betts and her husband, Clarence, contacted a wildlife expert they knew of. He said, "No problem. It will cost $60."

The next day Betts and Clarence went to watch the extraction from a safe distance out by the smokehouse. They report that the fellow walked right up to the cage, squatted down right by it, and began talking quietly to the skunk. Betts couldn't hear what he said, but after a few minutes, he slowly reached over and opened the cage door, and the skunk fled.

Then she heard the Skunk Whisperer yelling, "No. Oh, no. Don't go in there!"

From *Boomer* magazine, August-September 2015

And the skunk darted directly into the big groundhog hole beneath the house. Now both Punxsutawney Phil and Pepe Le Pew were living under the farmhouse.

"My sister is going to kill me," Betts told the Skunk Whisperer. "How will we know when these guys come out, so we can block up the hole?"

"Easy," says SW. "Just put a lot of flour on the ground and you'll see their footprints when they leave."

So Betts goes home, gets a five-pound bag of flour and spreads it around the opening of the groundhog hole. Before she can get back in her car, the skies open up. A deluge comes that would have disturbed Noah.

Betts calls us. "You have a backyard full of gravy," she says. "If we could catch this groundhog, we could have a heck of a Southern dinner."

Two weeks and FOUR captured groundhogs later, things are calm at the farmhouse. Pepe was never heard from again. We suspect he may have been voted out, for obvious reasons.

CHAPTER EIGHT

The Notorious Male Jerk Gene

RANDY: *Barbara Green, my colleague on* The Richmond News Leader *staff back in the 1980s, gets credit for discovering the aberrant "jerk gene" that only males possess.*

That is the gene that accounts for male appreciation of the Three Stooges and makes it impossible for men to ask directions. It causes us to leave wet towels on the bed and go deaf at will. It makes us wash the reds with the whites, and it leads us invariably to give the wrong answer when asked, "Do these pants make me look fat?"

I have written directly about my personal jerk gene in more than 25 columns; and it appears implicitly in hundreds more.

Is This the Jerk Gene at Work, or What?

You be the judge. Here's the story. Let's say there's a wife—could be anybody's wife, you understand—who ordinarily works from home but who has temporarily taken on a full-time job that keeps her at a desk on the other side of town all day. This new responsibility prevents the wife from keeping the house, especially the kitchen, up to its usual standards of straight/neat/clean.

Maybe this unknown wife's unknown husband who, heaven knows, would generally be out there helping with the straightening/neatening/cleaning is at a very busy time at his own job, so the housework has over the course of a month gotten a bit out of hand.

Pushed to the point of action, this conscientious wife and mother would get up at 4 a.m. Saturday to straighten/neaten/clean the kitchen before leaving at 6 for Charlottesville, to take her turn sitting with Uncle Roy, who is recovering from another heart attack.

For two hours in the early morning quiet, then, this unknown wife is washing dishes, scrubbing the kitchen floor, putting groceries in the proper cupboard, cleaning the fridge, scouring the stove, and otherwise tearing the kitchen apart and putting it back together.

Really getting into her task, unknown wife moves the kitchen table to the center of the room, finds some flowers to adorn it and a colorful rug to put beneath it.

From the *Richmond Times-Dispatch*, October 2, 1996

DOUGLAS PAYNE

Eventually, unknown husband wakes up, victim of a noisy dishwasher, and stumbles down the stairs, bleary-eyed and groggy. Then, as he scuffs into the kitchen, which last night at bedtime was a jungle of brown bags and dirty dishes and disarray, he makes the fatal mistake.

His first words, cast forth into the early-morning peace to be rued forever, are, "Why did you move the table?"

Now I ask you, was that so bad? If your very own spouse had walked in with that innocent observation, wouldn't you have kindly escorted him over to the coffeepot for caffeine and simply pointed out a few of the improvements you had wrought through diligent eforts while he slept peacefully upstairs?

The unknown wife, it must be reported, took another approach altogether in the version of the story I heard. The wife said—with, it might be noted, some volume and feeling—"That is the worst example of the jerk gene I've ever heard."

Some of you may recall that the jerk gene lies dormant in male bodies until confronted with occasions that call for good sense. It prevents us from being able to identify socks in the sock drawer and keys on the dresser top. It causes us to burp, or worse, when the wife is nearby talking on the phone. It accounts for fistfights in parking lots and dozing off at chick flics.

But is the incident reported above actually jerk gene? I think not. I believe that a man should be accorded impunity and immunity for the first thing that falls out of his mouth in the morning, even before he's had a cup of coffee and a honey bun.

Ah, but understanding seemed to be in short supply this day, so the unknown husband went back to bed to sleep through his wife's departure. Much later, on his second trip down to the kitchen, he was struck with how lovely it looked, sun streaming in freshly washed windows, flowers blooming on the table, everything neat and clean.

Fresh-brewed coffee was a sign that forgiveness had come, and with great pleasure he poured himself a cup and sat down to the morning paper, which kindly awaited him at his place. He rifled through the sections, the search confirming that the whole paper was there, except for the sports pages, which at that moment were in the back seat of an unknown car, halfway to Charlottesville.

BARB: *This column was in Randy's computer, but we have no idea when and where or even if it ran. We have no copy of it in print. It may have been one he later mined for parts.*

Chill Out!
It's Just the Jerk Gene
in Action

*B*arb no sooner got in the door and put her bottle of water in the fridge before saying, "What's that smell?"

What smell? Where? I didn't smell a thing.

Barb and Sarah had left Kyle and me home alone for a week while they went off to the beach with relatives. We fellows had a great time batching it, playing Putt-Putt one night and golf the next, leaving our shoes in the middle of the living room and totally giving ourselves over to the notorious male jerk gene.

In case you're unfamiliar with the jerk gene, it's the congenital masculine deficiency responsible for such distinctly male behaviorisms as an inability to find anything in your own home, a failure to notice your wife's new hairdo and the compulsion to wash everything in hot water.

Barb hadn't been gone 12 hours before a can of Coke that I had put in the freezer to chill exploded (BOOM!) like a pumpkin dropped on the front step, coating everything in the freezer with a thick layer of brown froth. Then Kyle dropped the top of an apparently fragile cookie jar into the porcelain sink. But the bad smell we knew nothing about.

I didn't hear any more about it until lunch. When

Barb got out the skim milk to have a glass with her sandwich, I saw her sniffing the air again. And when she tasted her milk, she said, "Yuck. I can't figure out what this tastes like but not milk."

My soda, sealed up in a can, tasted fine.

At supper, the tomato she'd sliced at lunch now tasted terrible, too. The butter was also weird. I was noticing these things myself, once she raised the issue. Even the bread tasted funny.

"Everything in this refrigerator is bad," Barb proclaimed. "Did the power go out while we were gone?"

No.

"Did you cook fish while I was gone?"

I thought back. Nope—didn't cook anything, as a matter of fact.

By Tuesday, Barb was going bonkers every time she opened the fridge. Out came the Ajax and a new box of baking soda. She removed everything from the fridge. At the back of the third shelf she found an open, half-eaten tin of sardines.

"Randy," she said to me, with a deep sigh, "You can't put unwrapped fish in the fridge. Everything in there absorbs that odor and taste."

Who knew? Nobody ever told me that before. I can't be held responsible if no one has told me. Like the time I took over washing the clothes and didn't find out for two months that dryers had lint filters. I see here not so much a jerk gene outbreak as a simple lack of information. Innocent mistakes were made.

One must remember that men are a work in progress. Until the medical profession finds a cure for the jerk gene, we'll always be leaving open cans of sardines in the fridge and exploding cans of Coke in the freezer and creating permanent brown stains on the front steps. I did mention that little incident with the pumpkin, didn't I?

BARB: *My own favorite jerk gene story does not involve Randy at all. It is about a young man named Kelly, the teenage son of our old friend Mary Bear. (Mary has, to her credit or shame, appeared in several columns with her own set of misadventures.) I'm sure Randy wrote about this somewhere, but here's my version. Kelly must be forgiven this incident because, at 16, clearly the jerk gene took him unawares.*

A Jerk Gene Prodigy
By Barb

Many years ago a short while after I made my switch from teaching to advertising, I threw a party and invited all my new friends in the business, Mary Bear among them. Mary was in the middle of a divorce and not yet dating.

"I don't want to come alone," she told me. "Would you mind if I brought Kelly?"

Kelly, one of her 16-year-old twin boys, looked and acted much older than his age and seemed to me to be pretty mature. So I said fine, although I was a little worried that he'd be totally bored. Ad people like to talk about advertising, and they like to talk to one another, so I felt sure it would be a short night for Mary's "date."

The evening went well. Mary and Kelly both seemed to be having fun. Being tall, blond and awfully cute, Kelly was getting a lot of attention from the women, and each time I passed by him he seemed to be holding up his end of the conversation just fine.

Sometime in the early morning hours, I noticed he had been spending a lot of time talking to a dark and hauntingly beautiful art director from another state, in town visiting one of my colleagues. She was probably at least twice his age. Leaning casually against the kitchen door frame, Kelly sipped his Coke. He and the woman, heads wreathed in smoke from her cigarette, looked like a GQ ad.

I paused to study them, feeling really proud that the young man was pulling this off so well and obviously having a great evening. It was sort of moving to note his amazing transition in one evening from the world of high school and sneakers to a real, live grown-up party.

Then as I headed to the kitchen and passed near them at the doorway, I overheard Kelly saying to his companion, in the smoothest sort of way, "Did you know that in this light, you have just the tiniest, teeniest mustache?"

CHAPTER NINE

The
Great Debate

BARB: *Randy and I have always thought we needed to write a book on Richmond's 1992 Presidential Debate because being behind the scenes for that, as we both were, was a college education and a trip to never-never land.*

As the Director of Public Relations at the University of Richmond for many years (his day job), Randy made the original contact with the Commission on Presidential Debates—an inquiry that led to UR's selection as host for that crucial '92 debate. And thanks to rampant nepotism, I was hired to run the debate office.

It turned out to be a fascinating and for many reasons historic debate. Many think it won that year's election for Bill Clinton. It certainly won a lot of attention here in Richmond where its iffy on-again/off-again status dominated the news for two months. Its economic and educational impact and the widespread local in-

117

volvement were good for a front-page article almost daily, week after week. Here are my a few of my impressions, some of which appeared in an article I wrote for the University of Richmond alumni magazine a few weeks after the debate was over.

The Running of the Pols
By Barb

*F*or the city, it meant jobs and publicity, excitement and community spirit, overbooked hotels and newspaper headlines. For Rand and me, the first 1992 Presidential Debate meant the hardest job and the most fun we'd ever had working together on a professional project. Our debate experience and inside stories gave rise to a lot of columns and articles, and a lot of speechmaking. In fact, every election cycle at debate time, as recently as the election of 2016, we were still being asked to talk about 1992.

The UR debate that year was the one to introduce the town hall format in which then-president George H.W. Bush, asked by an audience member, was unable to come up with the cost of a loaf of bread. Then, when the debate continued to go wrong for him (and no doubt wishing he were home in bed), he was caught looking at his watch by a TV audience of 110 million in the U.S. and tens of millions more around the world. That debate and that moment many think cost Bush his re-election and sent Bill Clinton on his way to the White House. It also provided Randy, me and the entire hard-working UR debate team an up-close and eye-opening education on politics and politicians.

We were almost immediately aware of a certain cut-throat approach in both the Democrat and Republican camps. We noticed that they waged war on each other in debate preparations but became united in trying to outmaneuver Ross Perot, the debate's third-party candidate, on matters large and small. An example of small: It was agreed that the selection of debate stools would be decided by compromise or majority rule, so the major party camps chose blue stools, really high ones, for the candidates to occupy on stage—with the result that while the over-six-foot-tall Bush and Clinton sat quite comfortably, the far shorter Ross Perot could only lean awkwardly against his.

The Dems and GOP also competed to have the most impressive motorcade as they arrived in town. The UR debate team was fielding questions like "How many cars do THEY have in their motorcade?" and "Do THEY have flags flying on their cars?" and "Are THEY being routed down Monument Avenue?" After all such decisions had been made, someone at UR realized that no one had contacted Ross Perot to learn what his motorcade should be. A team member called him up, and Perot answered the phone himself. He was told about the preparations for the arrival in town of his political opponents and was asked what he desired. In his folksy Texas accent, he said, "Awl I need is a rental car and a road map." It was almost enough to make you vote for him.

Many of the top national reporters showed up for the event, as did a number of name-brand politicians. To name a couple, Tom Brokaw, Brit Hume and John Chancellor were in town and working, as were Joe Biden, John Kerry and James Carville. Of course, Barbara Bush and Hillary Clinton got a lot of attention, too. Celebrities were all around.

The response in the city was overwhelming. The Debate Office lined up more than 1,000 volunteers, and probably another thousand called in after opportunities were already gone. Hotel rooms from Richmond to Williamsburg were filled. Twenty new cars were loaned by various dealerships, and 75 television sets were borrowed. A hundred miles of cable were laid, 200 telephones installed, 100,000

Barb came off looking good on the front page of the *Times-Dispatch*,
not quite as good in her husband's column inside the paper

copies made—and Randy opened "Good Morning, America," sitting on one of those tall blue stools, on the day of the debate.

An old cabbie told us he had never had so much business as he did during that week. He also told the story of another cabbie who had picked up a major news personality at the airport. She had said to him, "I'm here for the debate. Take me to the University of Virginia." The enterprising fellow did just that—140 miles round trip.

We enjoyed the skills of a Jimmy Dean impersonator who called the debate office to suggest handing out sausage-on-a-stick to the town hall audience during the debate. That audience, by the way, was selected randomly by the Gallup organization. Their people had cold-called not just the 209 people who actually could be accommodated, but 325 in total, to make sure all seats were filled. Many of the extras who were turned away ended up out front of the arena, picketing for the TV cameras with signs saying "Debate Reject."

In addition to the chosen 209 (excluding the one who turned up inebriated), two others showed up claiming they had been called by God.

My favorite personal debate moment was the day I picked up the morning paper to see my picture in the debate office, in living color, on the front page. I was pretty pleased until I turned to Randy's column and read, along with everyone else in the city, that due to our long hours working on the debate, our temporary wave-as-you-pass lifestyle and the resulting disorganization at home, "Barb was unable to find her brush this morning and had to resort to using the dog comb."

CHAPTER TEN

Bad Things, Good People

BARB: *We figure that altogether, Rand may have written about 2,000 columns, maybe more, over 30 years—and he's still writing a regular column for* Boomer *magazine. Most of those columns are humorous ones, pleasant stories of family and community life, many containing letters and stories from readers.*

But there are a couple of categories of columns that don't fit Randy's typical subject matter or tone. He has rarely written negatively of people or companies that aggrieve him. He doesn't usually write about tragedies, disasters or mayhem. He seldom writes anything designed to instruct (unless you count the three or four pieces about leeches—he really got smitten with leeches for a while there).

Sometimes national tragedies or disasters were too impactful not to discuss, so Randy did write of 9/11, of Katrina, of Iraq and other wars. He wrote several times about the O.J. Simpson trial. His sister, Linda, was at that time a domestic abuse counselor and contributed mightily to those columns. Her insights and experiences provoked a strong reader response. We were stunned (Linda was not) with the number of domestic abuse victims who wrote in to share their stories.

Only in two cases we could recall has Randy written of dire tragedies close to home. In one instance, time distanced the reader a bit from the horror; in the other there was no solace, but the effect on the city was so pronounced and so personal that attention must be paid.

Encounter with a Murderer

So far as I know, I have come face to face with only one cold-blooded murderer in my life, and as I write this more than 30 years later, it's not a memory I much like to recall.

In late summer 1961, right after Barb and I were married, we were working the tail end of a summer job in Charlottesville before moving to Richmond for the start of my junior year at UR. The job involved traveling to courthouses all over Virginia to search deed books for a particular piece of information our lawyer employer needed for a client.

One day found us at the Spotsylvania County courthouse, where Barb sat at a table taking notes while I went

From the *Richmond Times-Dispatch*, January 27, 1993

back and forth to the shelves delivering to her the heavy deed books. On one of my trips away from the table, Barb—bent over her work—suddenly had a sensation of fear. The hair on the back of her neck stood up, she said, exactly the way she'd always read about in novels.

When she looked up, she faced the icy eyes of a man seated across the table from her, and at that moment, she thought the hair on her head stood up as well. I had a similar reaction when, on my way back with another deed book, I saw the same shackled and handcuffed man as he was led from the Clerk's Office into the adjacent courtroom, obviously about to face trial.

When I got to Barb's table, I asked, "Who in God's name was that?" And she, shaking her head and looking a little pale, said, "I have no idea, but I hope never to see him again."

My lawyer here in Richmond, Andy Wood, who has been called upon to defend many a murderer, has told me on several occasions that most murderers are just like the rest of us, in those moments when they're not murdering. He often finds them polite, worried about their mothers, anxious about the future and truly sorry that in one wretched moment they lost control and made a terrible choice. But then there's Melvin Davis Rees.

Melvin Davis Rees is the man who in 1959 murdered Carroll Jackson, his wife, Mildred, and their two children, Susan, 5, and Janet, 17 months. The Louisa family had stopped to help a stranger whose car appeared to be broken down on a country road. It was a chilling story. The whole family had just disappeared on Sunday evening, January 11, leaving their car on the side of the road, keys in the ignition, dolls and purse and baby bottles on the seats.

For almost two months, people in that area were frightened and frustrated. Then, on May 4, Mr. Jackson's body was discovered in a brush pile near Fredericksburg, clothed in his blue Sunday suit, hands tied behind his back with his own red necktie. He had been shot in the head.

When police turned him over, baby Janet lay suffocated beneath him. A little more than two weeks later, the bodies of Mrs. Jackson and little Susan were unearthed from a shallow grave in Maryland.

Rees was arrested after an acquaintance told police he had reason to believe Rees had committed those crimes. A search of his parents' home in Hyattsville, Md., produced the revolver that killed Mr. Jackson and a journal recounting the family's kidnapping and murders. One entry read, "Drove to select area & killed husband and baby. Now the mother and daughter are all mine."

The day we encountered this nightmare of a human being, the clerk at the courthouse desk soon enlightened us that the man on trial that day was the accused murderer of Carroll Jackson. As unlikely as it seems, the deputies had deposited him for a few minutes in the only available chair in the Clerk's Office, the one directly opposite my wife.

I've been a liberal for much of my life, but one way in which I sometimes deviate from the liberal line is to allow on occasion an acceptance of capital punishment. That philosophy was enhanced after a brief encounter in a courthouse in Spotsylvania.

The Spotsylvania jury sentenced Rees to death after 28 minutes of deliberation, but the Supreme Court saved him. Today, declared legally insane, he is in maximum security at the U. S. Medical Center for Federal Prisoners in Springfield, Mo. And that's still not far enough away for me.

[Note: Rees was eventually connected to at least nine murders. He died in prison in 1995.]

A Chill
to the Heart

Considering that I never met them, never saw them, I have thought about them so many times over the past months and years. What happened to them has changed a lot of lives around this city, including mine, in quiet and meaningful ways.

On many a weekend morning when life is leisurely, Barb and I will get up and open the front door to find a clear, warm, promising day. One of us will step out and get the paper. Then we'll start pulling the sections we want to read as we head for the sofa, to settle back, safe and secure and inviolate in our home, our haven.

Inevitably, within a few minutes, one of us will put down the paper, get up and walk back over to the door, and check to make sure the storm door is locked.

That's just one of the legacies of the Harvey family murders two years ago this month. Before the Harveys were murdered on January 1, 2006—and "murdered" is not a strong enough word for what happened to that family— we would never have thought to be concerned about an unlocked door on a Sunday morn.

In 20 years of column-writing, rarely have I dwelt on the sad or horrendous events of life. I prefer to help people smile, to spread a little joy, but sorrow and even tragedy are part of life, too, and we can't pretend grief doesn't come to all of us—for some in larger and more horrific doses than for others. To many Richmonders—the isolated old, the poor, the homeless, persecuted minorities and all those in crime-ridden neighborhoods—fear is often a huge part of daily life. I can't imagine.

Every city has its unforgettable, unfathomable crimes, crimes so heinous that they shake up an entire community and linger as part of a city's story for years, long after the victims are laid to rest. These are the crimes you can't get out of your mind, the ones that frighten you until the guilty are caught—and often long after. Thoughts of these crimes resurface each time you drive past a particular house or down a particular street. When you pass through a certain neighborhood with an out-of-town visitor in your car, you might say, "That store right there is where . . ." or "That's the house where. . . . "

During my era in Richmond, the Harvey murders, the Southside Strangler, and the Briley brothers' crime spree seem to have inspired the most fear and horror in the areas where I live and work. Those cases bring a chill to the heart and a jolt to the soul, and the Harvey case, because of the lost children, is especially haunting.

As a husband and father, there are details of that case that I never want to know, images that my mind can't bear to imagine, and yet, unbidden, sometimes they come. And so it is that, particularly on sunny, promising, inviting, unseasonably warm January mornings when I want to leave my front door open and welcoming, I don't.

Often, then, I say a quick prayer for this man and wife that I never knew, who had to bear far more than should be asked of any human—a prayer for them and for their two little girls. It is also a prayer for all of us, a wish that no one else will ever again have to bear the unbearable. It's a prayer that can never be realized.

And so we lock the door, as if that could keep out evil, as if stronger wood or better locks will save us, rather than a far-reaching change in the human heart.

It is another January now that the Harvey family will miss, another new year with promises denied, when nothing is assured, when nothing can be taken for granted. I hope this year to let them go—Bryan, Kathryn, Stella and Ruby—to focus not on their deaths but on the beautiful things I learned about them from newspaper stories and their friends: about their kind natures, their civic-mindedness and social consciousness, their love of fellow man, their joyous enthusiasm for life, their promise. I will try to remember them this way.

But I will continue to lock the door.

RANDY: *Family stories can't always be happy ones, either. These three stand out for me because there was so much pain involved for all our family as we helplessly watched or waited.* Boomer *magazine ran the next story alongside a feature on financial elder abuse.*

A Widow at Risk
A true story of a charming stranger and a lonely woman with money

She met him online, chatted electronically for two weeks, then invited him to journey 1,000 miles to Virginia and move in—but this is not a Valentine's story by any means.

She's nearly 80 years old, a lonesome widow living alone for several years in her own home in a small town in central Virginia, with no blood relatives nearby to look out for her. Some relatives by marriage do call and email, but they, too, live at some distance.

When she invited her newfound love into her home,

From *Boomer* magazine, February-March 2010

she knew very little about him. He was about her age, coming off a bad divorce, with three grown children—two of whom he spoke to.

He knew a lot about her. She had told him. She owned her home, had a little money saved and had just inherited about $70,000 from her mother. He asked her to send him $4,000 to pay off his bills and cover the cost of his trip to Virginia. She sent it promptly.

When she excitedly told her neighbors that he was on his way, they cautioned her about him. And when she reported those admonitions to him, he said to tell them she didn't need them anymore, that he would be looking after her from now on. That's what she told the one who had cut her grass for years and the one who came over each morning to put the brace on her leg.

Within days of his arrival, she bought him an expensive, top-of-the-line riding mower, a pre-assembled storage shed and a two-wheeled trailer, one of the big ones requiring a license plate.

He said her TV was too small to watch, so she bought the largest screen high-def TV they could find. He thought the kitchen table was the wrong shape, so she bought a rectangular one. He decided he wanted a Chevy van, so she purchased one. Then he suggested major renovations to the house, closing up the inside stairs to the basement to give more space, and planning a complete renovation of the kitchen.

She bought him a chain saw and a variety of tools, and he ordered a big metal garage from Minnesota and hired some locals to assemble it—the same fellows who would install the roof now needed over the outside basement steps.

The house was cluttered, he said; they needed to sell some stuff. When someone bought a hundred-dollar item at the sale, she handed over the money to him. Meanwhile, he packed up boxes of items from the house to send to his grown children.

Soon he was answering her telephone and staying close at hand as she talked to her old in-laws and friends.

Two months after he arrived, the widow married him and added his name to her lease.

She has been very careful as to what she tells the relatives, mostly sharing excitement about this man who has suddenly "added so much motion" to her life. "There's always something going on," she says.

When people ask if they can visit, she asks him if it's OK. Two who have met him describe him as "sort of British-looking and charming." They were less charmed when a family member found out that his ex-girlfriend back in the faraway state had taken out a personal protection order against him.

What is to be done about those who get foolish as they get old? How do we keep them safe? We can make sure seniors get their flu shots, put good locks on their doors and give them an emergency-alert pendant. But how do we protect them from the dangers of cyberspace, especially when they're eager to make themselves vulnerable?

There's no way to ensure protection online, and no alarm that can be raised in this case will be heard. Those who care about her tread lightly. They don't want her to cut ties, leaving her alone in the hands of a stranger.

The end is out there somewhere. It may turn out well or it may be a disaster. We can only wait and watch.

RANDY: The follow-up to that column came two years later, in February-March 2012. When I first wrote these, I did not identify the lady involved as a relative because I wanted to protect her privacy. But she was one of us by marriage, and I wish we could have done more to protect her.

The Rest of the Story

*E*xactly two years ago I wrote of an aging widow who had met online a man who captured her fancy, invited him to move to Virginia, and in short order married him. Those of us who cared about her were aghast and fearful. She had been showing mild signs of confusion after an illness but was of presumably sound mind, so there was nothing to be done. We tried. We talked to her, to her local social services office and the local police. We traced him online and learned that there was a protective order against him in his home state.

So we knew this guy was not wonderful, and he caught her at a time when two people she cared deeply about—her longtime boyfriend and her mother—had just died, and she was vulnerable and sad.

When we told her we were worried, she said she'd be fine, told us of her inheritances and added that she had a couple hundred thousand in savings, plus a pretty sizeable pension from a long-held job. I suppose she told him all that as well.

Before he came, she had owned her beautiful home free and clear. There she had outlived two husbands and her longtime boyfriend. Counting her Social Security, she had been in excellent financial shape to see her through the rest of her life.

As I write this follow-up column, she hasn't got a penny.

It didn't take long for every dollar to be spent, much of it on fanciful, impulse purchases like a hot tub they used only once, two unneeded walk-in bathtubs and expensive

From *Boomer* magazine, February-March 2012

high-def TVs. They bought two pedigreed dogs that they weren't up to walking, and when the fine hardwood floors were ruined, he had carpet installed atop them. The dogs soon ruined that, too.

He started about half a dozen unfinished projects, all to the detriment of the house. And when the cash was all gone, he got a reverse mortgage. Decisions were made overnight. The house was on the market before anyone knew it, and he announced they were moving back to his home state. Virginia was a terrible place. People were unfriendly and were all "in it for what they could get out of you."

To finance the move, they cashed in her pension, held an auction, and took a loss. He sent the cash from the house sale to a sister back home, who was to buy a small house for them, presumably in his name. And so they moved, over 1,000 miles away where the lady, now in her 80s, knows no one and where we can no longer keep an eye on her.

She called to say goodbye, apprehensive but determined to make the best of things. She had said in the past that while he wasn't physically abusive, he was often verbally and emotionally abusive. "Never in my life has anyone called me the names he does," she said.

Barb asked whether she regretted taking him in. "Sometimes I do," she said. "I just didn't want to spend the last years of my life alone."

EPILOGUE

Shortly before this column went to press and one month after she arrived at her new home, we received word that the lady had died of a brain aneurysm. The husband called, saying he had had her cremated and asking if anyone "down there" wanted to buy the two burial plots she had owned back in Virginia. "She left me," he said, "saddled with a world of debt."

The Day We Lost Brenda

I hunted for at least seven months to find a specific gift this Christmas that was a half-century overdue. When I finally came across it and shipped it in the mail to Arkadelphia, Ark., I felt as though I had finally put some kind of personal closure to one of my family's saddest stories.

I was one of three siblings and seven first cousins who all pretty much grew up together in Charlottesville in the late '40s, early '50s. All our dads were brothers and all the moms took turns raising us, as all the grown-ups in each household worked in various family restaurants night and day. The youngest cousin was Brenda, the daughter of my Dad's youngest brother, and she, being the baby, was everybody's favorite. We seven rapscallions spent hours playing cowboys and Indians and games made up on the spot on any beautiful summer day.

Then when Brenda was five years old, she and her mother disappeared, vanished overnight.

The mother, secretly pregnant by a man not my uncle, took Brenda via a circuitous route to Atlanta. There she had her baby and some months later abandoned them both in the tiny apartment where they had been living. Brenda recalls trying to feed and care for Baby Lorna, whom she adored, but she doesn't recall how long they were in that place alone. Eventually someone discovered them, the police came, and both were taken away to an orphanage.

Meanwhile, Brenda's father returned to his parents' home in Arkansas and searched for Brenda as best he could, with no idea where she and her mother might be. When he tracked her down at the orphanage months later, Brenda remembers coming forward for a jubilant reunion with him, only to hear him say of the little sister whose hand she held, "That one is not mine."

So Brenda lost her mother, her six cousins, her baby sister, her home, and what she had known as her life before she was even old enough to start school. Within another year or so, her dad, unable to care for her and apparently too ashamed to let any of the Charlottesville family know, put Brenda up for adoption.

In 1989, about 30 years after I had last seen her, Brenda came back into my life. What a blessing to find she had been adopted by a childless couple and had grown up in a good home. Now the wife of a Baptist preacher and the mother of three, she was ready to track down her original family, including the mother who had walked away and left her. So she and her husband, Lee, came to Virginia, reunited with her cousins, and went to Crozet for a most interesting reunion with her birth mother.

As you can imagine, there are lots of stories here, and Brenda has put them down in a manuscript that she hopes to publish some day. In that manuscript I found the paragraph that led to my hunt for a specific Christmas present, a memory from our childhood together.

"We didn't have a lot of cowboy and Indian props," she wrote of her days playing with her cousins, "except for one coonskin cap, and Randy, being the oldest, got to be the one to wear it. I thought he looked mighty important wearing that furry cap with its long tail swinging down the back of his neck. I so much wanted to wear it, even for just a little bit, but I knew trying to sell him on equal wearing time would be impossible. I never knew which aunt or uncle was responsible for providing just one coonskin cap for seven children, but I'm sure it was the cause of lots of battles among the cousins for years to come."

Little Brenda in her early happy years in Charlottesville, with Randy's mother, Beth, and the family dog, Laddie.

If it was, Brenda missed those battles. She missed so much, and the rest of us did as well because Brenda is now one of the dearest people I've ever met. My brother and sister and their spouses, along with Barb and me, all got to spend a full week with Brenda and Lee in Arkansas this year, so that reunion was my favorite Christmas gift. And mine to her, thanks to the Tennessee Welcome Center Gift Shop, was a soft, silky, ring-tailed coonskin cap.

CHAPTER ELEVEN

Hail, Brittania

Did I Ever Tell You About the Time I Met the Queen?

I wasn't able to get out to see Queen Elizabeth when she was in Williamsburg, but there was a time years ago when Her Majesty passed my way, looked directly upon me and bestowed a lovely smile and, I think, a slight nod. I like the queen.

My "meeting" with her came in 1972 when Barb and I were living in London for a while as I finished writing my Ph.D dissertation. That happened to be the year the queen and Prince Philip celebrated their silver wedding anniversary with a walkabout—on Nov. 20, according to the journal I kept that year.

Barb and I learned of the walkabout plans late the

From *City Edition*, May 14, 2007

night before, so we got up early, caught the tube from Shepherd's Bush where we were living, and soon found ourselves behind a rope in the financial district (which is called the City), along with everyone else in London.

People lined both sides of the street about 20 deep, but thanks to our early arrival, we were on the rope. That was a huge advantage when the royals passed. They were all there—not just Her Majesty and Prince Philip but Princess Margaret and her Lord Snowden, the queen mother, Prince Charles and Princess Anne.

The queen was far lovelier than I had expected, warmer looking than in her pictures. I turn to Barb's journal for an accurate description because we guys don't record details like this: "The queen wore an aquamarine coat dress with mink at the collar and cuffs. She had quite nice skin and lovely blue eyes. Her makeup was perfect. She had a '50s hairdo and a purposeful manner, almost as though she really wanted to walk up to someone and talk but wasn't sure whom to pick out."

Princess Anne had no trouble making that decision. She chose me. I still don't believe it after all these years, but in a crowd shoulder to shoulder for miles, Princess Anne walked directly over to me, stopped and asked, "Are you American?"

I was dumbfounded, literally speechless for a few seconds. Barb, standing at my side, found her voice first and said, "Yes, we are." Anne never looked her way, never acknowledged her presence or response, but kept her eyes on me until I stammered a repeat of Barb's confirmation.

We later learned that one does not speak to royalty unless directly spoken to, and Princess Anne knew the rule even if we didn't. She continued to talk only to me, asking what I was doing in London, and when I told her I was doing research on William Faulkner's literary reputation in Britain, she indicated she was familiar with his work.

My journal records that she also asked where else we

DOUGLAS PAYNE

had been besides London, and in response to my list of all the places we had visited in England, she said, "Ah, you're traveling about then."

The whole thing seemed like a long conversation to me, but when Barb and I excitedly reconstructed it on the way home on the bus, we saw that it was actually pretty brief.

"How do you suppose she knew I was American?" I wondered.

"Maybe she caught your accent when you yelled, 'Hey, Queenie!'" Barb suggested.

We had a second round of excitement that night when our good friends from Wales called to say they had seen us "on the telly with the queen." Sure enough, the BBC had recorded the queen's nod to us and Anne's conversation with me, and it ran a number of times on newscasts that evening and the next day. We called the BBC and tried to get a copy, but they wouldn't or couldn't provide it, so you'll have to take my word for it.

Actually, Barb did have our movie camera and was filming as the royal family approached us, but once Anne came so near, it was rude to stick the camera in her face and Barb put it down.

That night, we called my parents back in Charlottesville, hoping we might also turn up on CBS, but we didn't. They were quite excited with our story, though. I knew my dad was going to enjoy having this tale to share at the Elks Club because he always grumbled about the outrageous tall tales the other guys there were always telling. "They're constantly exaggerating," he'd say. "Nobody would believe half the stuff they tell."

After we returned to the states and had occasion months later to accompany Dad to his club, imagine my surprise when his friends gathered around and asked me to tell them all about my visit with the queen and Prince Philip at Buckingham Palace.

The Leech Gatherer

*I*f you're the kind of person who recoiled with Humphrey Bogart as he frantically tore the hungry leeches from his body in "The African Queen," you might want to put down your morning waffle before continuing. But if you like a good medical pioneer story, stick with me here.

About every 10 years I write something about my good friend Dr. Roy Sawyer. I couldn't forget Roy if I wanted to because his name and photo keep turning up in unexpected places. Twice now as I've been reading *Time* or *Newsweek*, I turn a page and there's Roy. I've come upon him in *People*, as well as the *The New York Times* and the *The Washington Post*. Once as I was driving home from work listening to NPR, I heard about some guy who was at that very moment sailing down the Amazon River in search of *Haementeria ghilianii*, better known as the Giant Amazon Leech. It had to be Roy.

Roy, who was born in Tidewater Virginia, has lived in Wales for most of his life with his delightful Welsh wife, Lorna. The two of them, along with daughter Bethany, run Biopharm, a very successful leech-breeding business near Swansea that raises, sells and ships leeches to doctors, hospitals and medical schools all over the world. Roy is a foremost world authority on leeches and their use for medicinal purposes. (See his three-volume opus, "Leech Biology and Behavior," which might well have been subtitled "Everything You Ever Wanted to Know about Leeches—and More.")

Excerpted from *The Richmond News Leader*, December 7-8, 1988, and the *Richmond Times-Dispatch*, July 12, 1995, and September 3, 2005

Hail, Brittania

His favorite leech, the *Hirudo medicinalis*, comes with the perfect mouth parts for sucking blood from mammals (i.e., you and me. And better you than me.).

Of course, what you and I remember first about leeches is all the men who were notoriously bled with leeches while dying, including Lord Byron and Stalin. (OK, we don't care about Stalin.)

And you're right, George Washington was also bled—but not with leeches. Nobody uses leeches to bleed dying patients anymore; however, the little suckers are in strong demand for microsurgery applications. Leech saliva has anti-clotting properties second to none, and a leech or two can keep blood flowing through the tiniest veins, to help

Dr. Roy Sawyer with his leeches.
(Randy claims the biologist is one of his saner friends.)

141

restore normal circulation to a reattached body part, like an ear or a finger, allowing it to return to perky life.

Leech saliva even comes with its own anesthetic, so the process is painless. Roy's method of finding them, if I remember correctly from a visit he paid once to a creek near my farmhouse at Keswick, was simply to wade out in the water like a giant piece of bait, slosh around and then head to the bank to check for a catch. (Believe it or not, Roy is one of my saner friends.)

Despite the valuable contributions of the leech in recent years, Roy has had to work hard to return them to favor after their overuse in the early 1800s to treat everything from colds to nymphomania. (I don't have any specifics there.)

We got a full tour of Biopharm when we were in Wales recently. There was something a little incongruous about beautiful Bethany Sawyer strolling us among the various tanks and jars full of dark brown slimy creatures with extremely strong jaws as though she were exhibiting colorful koi.

She shared stories, too, of the day Prince Charles visited the lab. The prince spent an afternoon there and seemed fascinated with the care and feeding of the leeches, but she said he did check his "trouser turn-ups" at the end of his visit.

And when one little leech escaped the tank and hungrily danced around the floor at the prince's feet, no doubt in search of quality blue blood, the prince responded by giving it the royal stamp of approval.

Meet the Tates

*L*ast Friday Barb and I took Sir Saxon Tate and his Lady Virginia to lunch at the Smokey Pig in Ashland.

The Fitzgeralds don't often get the chance to dine with nobility—this was the first time, actually—and perhaps the Smokey Pig seems an unlikely choice for welcoming to town members of the family that founded the Tate Gallery in London.

Ginny Tate is a Winchester native, and we reckoned that after almost 40 years of living abroad in Paris and London, she might be ready for a rack of ribs and a look at Ashland—which is, after all, "the center of the universe."

My Barb and Ginny became dear and lifelong friends when they were Bobbi Goodman and Ginny Sturm in their undergraduate days at what was then Longwood College in the 1960s. In fact, "Bobbi" (as her college friends still call her) was Ginny's big sister there.

I knew Ginny pretty well, too, because she was kind enough to go out with some of my wild and crazy fraternity brothers when I'd drive over from Richmond to date Barb.

We always knew Ginny was destined for an interesting life. Sometimes you can just tell.

After her graduation in 1964, Ginny, a French major, went on to graduate school at the University of Kentucky for her master's degree and some Ph.D. work. Then, when her fiancé was killed in a plane crash, she picked up and moved to Paris, where she taught English for several years.

On the flight over, she happened to be seated next

From the *Richmond Times-Dispatch*, November 12, 2003

to a dashing Englishman who, with proper British reserve, didn't speak a word to her until she, with proper American boldness, initiated a conversation that went on all across the Atlantic.

That gentleman was Sir Saxon Tate, and the two struck up a friendship that became a courtship that became a wonderful marriage. The result has been a storybook life for Miss Ginny Sturm from Winchester, Va., and—knowing Ginny—no doubt a lively and continually fascinating life for her husband as well.

(When Barb and I were growing up in Charlottesville, nearby in Greenwood was the home of the famous Lady Nancy Langhorne Astor, another beautiful American woman who had gone abroad, fallen in love and married a noble.

(Lady Astor was party to a famous exchange—perhaps apocryphal, but I hope not—with Winston Churchill. She told him with some irritation at a party that if she were married to him, she would poison his coffee. He replied, "And if I were married to you, I would drink it.")

Ginny, who also travels in some very interesting social circles, seemingly is unfazed by her rarefied life.

Despite a lifestyle that includes homes in London and Portugal and constant travel to exotic places, Ginny was never content to be simply "M'Lady." She founded and ran for 15 years the largest and most successful recruitment agency in London, retiring only recently to enjoy more fully her family and the opportunities life and hard work have brought to her.

She is as dear, as witty and as sharp as we remembered her, though her familiarity with barbecue places may have slipped a bit. As she and Barb planned this reunion at the Smokey Pig, Ginny emailed such questions as "Do they serve wine?" and "Do we need reservations?"

"Ginny's been away for a good while," Barb chuckled.

Hail, Brittania

Anyway, lunch was perfect. Sir Saxon and Lady Tate marveled at the food and service, saying they could really tell they were back in the hospitable South. We were meeting him for the first time, somewhat nervously, since he has the hereditary title of baronet and was awarded a CBE (Commander of the British Empire) by the Queen. He was a delight—a fascinating, good-humored man with many entertaining stories of his 50 years of traveling worldwide for his sugar refining business.

After lunch, Ginny and Saxon went on to their quarters at The Jefferson. I went back to work, and Barb returned home to the boring task of sorting through things for her weekend yard sale.

"I hope you don't feel cheated with the life you've had," I told her later on the phone. "If you want to pretend, though, feel free to call me 'my lord' anytime you want."

"Married to you," she said, "I'm far more likely to be saying 'Oh my lord!'"

[Note: Sadly, Sir Saxon Tate died in July of 2012.]

145

The Bickersons

Barb and I had dinner with the Bickersons last week, which I thought I would mention since you know them, too. Everyone knows the Bickersons, though maybe not by that name.

That's the couple that can't resist the urge to pick at each other or outright argue some little domestic difference during an otherwise pleasant evening with friends. Our recent Bickersons, like all of them, are lovely people who probably aren't even aware they have this little problem, but the rest of us certainly are.

This night their "discussion" was about her tendency to pull the car too far up onto the grass at the end of the driveway, and she responded by pointing out his tendency to correct and finish her stories for her.

When we got home, we were exhausted, so I settled onto the sofa to relax with my book for a few minutes. Almost immediately, Barb, who abhors overhead lights, came along and switched on a table lamp near me and cut off the overhead.

I, in turn, got up and cut the overhead back on and switched off the lamp. "I don't see how you read with an overhead," she said from the doorway.

"I like it," I said.

"It's hard on your eyes," she said.

"I like it," I said.

"That's a smaller-watt bulb up there," she said.

"I like it," I said.

From the *Richmond Times-Dispatch*, February 6, 1997

Hail, Brittania

"Doesn't the glare bother you?" she asked.

"I like it," I said.

"Give over," she said, which made me laugh.

It brought back memories of the English couple who occupied the next flat during the time Barb and I lived in London in the early 1970s. Being separated from them only by a thin wall was like sitting down with one of those British sitcoms on PBS. After the first week or so, we didn't even feel ashamed for listening. They were that good.

Mrs. Bickerson was a very logical debater. She came to the arguments well prepared, went down her list point by point, and laid out her side of the evening's disagreement

DOUGLAS PAYNE

with passion.

But every time she paused for a breath, Mr. Bickerson, whom we on the other side of the wall imagined sitting calmly in his armchair reading *The Times* during her tirade, would simply and quietly say, "Give over."

"Give over" (pronounced "oh-vah") just meant "give it up. Admit you're wrong." But like Bickersons the world over, neither ever did, whether the issue was the neighbor's right to park his lorry in front of their flat or the wife's having given the husband's old jacket to the "rag-and-bone man."

After we'd lived in our flat for several months, our landlady one day invited us down for lunch with her and her husband. They lived in the downstairs part of the house, and we had seen very little of them during our stay. Our association prior to this lunch had consisted of greetings as we passed in the front hall and a few pleasantries exchanged as we turned over the rent to one or the other of them each month.

It was not the most comfortable lunch I've ever had. They were lovely people but quite reserved, and soon we fell into a bit of a silence. To get things going again, I started to tell them about the hilarious adventures of the Bickersons next door. They were very interested and asked a number of questions about things we had overheard.

A few days later, returning from a walk to the neighborhood grocery, I looked up to see Barb sitting in the bay window in our bedroom. I had my hand half-raised to wave when, to my horror, I saw that in the window to her right, which should have been the Bickersons' flat, my landlady was shaking out a dust mop.

I realized instantly that while she and her husband lived downstairs by day, a back stairway must have led to their bedroom upstairs, on the other side of the thin wall where Barb and I had spent so many nights enjoying their arguments.

Hail, Brittania

Shortly afterward, Barb and I decided to move on to Wales for a while and our landlords did not seem all that sad to see us go.

MARVA NOVITZ

Randy and Barb on their romantic gondola ride ... pre-pigeon.

150

CHAPTER TWELVE

On the Road Again

BARB: *One of our greatest pleasures has been travel, especially in recent years with the kind assistance of our travel-savvy cousins Marva and Norm from New Jersey. They have visited every continent including Antarctica, and there could be no better guides. Last year they led us to Venice, and life was complete! This description of our gondola ride is from my travel journal, reprinted as part of Randy's Boomer column, "The Great Adventure Continues."*

Love Boat

The culmination of the trip in more ways than one was our gondola ride. That's what everyone does in Venice, of course, and it's something you never think you'll get to do when growing up on a farm at Keswick. But here we were on our last night in Venice, and our romantic gondola ride would be something to remember always. The gondoliers are garbed in very distinctive striped shirts and straw hats, and the most romantic gondolas have either blue or red velvet interiors. We got a blue one, settled in, and drifted lazily through the narrow canals of this great city.

The sights were window boxes with colorful flowers, little arched bridges of all shapes and designs, just high enough for the standing gondolier to pass below, a house where Mozart had visited (hear the piano?) and white doves on the eaves. I was aware of water lapping against the foundations of ancient buildings, the bells of St. Marks in the distance, soft voices wafting across narrow alleyways, the occasional bird call or a moment of laughter from an open window. The sun was about to set, with that incredible Venetian light, and it was as romantic and serene a moment as life can provide.

Our gondolier at some point began to talk softly in his beautiful Italian—I felt sure he was reciting poetry to us because of his tone and inflections.* Remembering the legend that if you kiss beneath one of the bridges, you will return to Venice, we leaned in to ensure our return as we approached one that was particularly lovely—and a pigeon crapped exactly on the center of my forehead!

To complete the romantic end of an unbelievable first visit to Venice, the gondolier said, 'Issa gud et notta seagull. Den you needa da shower.'

[*BARB: Randy says our gondolier was actually talking on his cell phone.]

Scent of a Snake

DOUGLAS PAYNE

I met a man once—his first name was Massie—who could smell snakes.

We were standing near a woodpile at his house in Fluvanna County, and when I took a few steps over to sit down on it as we talked, Massie said, "I wouldn't do that, if I was you. Smelled a snake under there this morning."

Sure you did, I thought, but I moved back where I started, to humor him. And a few minutes later a snake roughly the size of my leg (an impressive circumference, even in those days), slithered out from the other side of the woodpile and headed for the creek.

I'm a believer. If we'd had Massie with us the only time I ever got Barb out on a golf course, she probably wouldn't have stepped against the water moccasin and cut short a promising career on the links. She and the snake quickly gave new meaning to the old golfing term "strokes," as they each just about had one.

"What does a snake smell like?" I asked Massie that day. (This was right after I gave up trying to learn to play the harmonica, and I thought I needed to develop another talent. Snake smelling seemed like a possibility.)

From the *Richmond Times-Dispatch*, March 22, 1995

Massie thought about it a few minutes and then said, "They smell yellow."

I'm sure that's exactly what they smell like, but that instruction was about as useful as my friend Richard Rankin's advice had been about taking up the harmonica: "There's only 10 holes in the thing, Randy," he said. "How hard can it be?"

I don't know why I ever doubted old Massie could smell snakes. He was, after all, a distant cousin of my wife, and a lot of her kinfolk are kind of colorful and interesting like that. There's another one who can divine water. A good many of them are walking Southern short stories.

So far as I know, though, no one else in Barb's family can sniff out snakes, though her mother could smell rain and snow. My sweet little mother-in-law would step out in the yard on the sunniest day you ever saw and say, "Rain's coming—I smell it." And if you had any sense, you'd go back and get your umbrella right then.

I also recall clear, cold winter mornings when she'd say, "We'd better get to the grocery store. There's a smell of snow in the air." And in a few hours the sky would turn gray and down would come flakes thicker than Kellogg's.

Anyway, I was doing some thinking about senses of smell the other day, mainly because mine is generally pretty poor. The workers in my ol' factory went out on strike some years back. I can't even smell the broiler when I leave it on, or Barb's latest perfume.

So it occurred to me that maybe the ability to smell is two-thirds a matter of concentrating and focusing on something. The more harried and hectic my life gets, the less I seem to be able to smell.

Thirty miles this side of Virginia Beach, Barb will say, "Oh, can you just smell that ocean!" And I, fighting the traffic and dreading the tunnel, smell only exhaust fumes.

As I took a little walk around the block on one of those gloriously beautiful days last weekend, I decided to concentrate on smells, but I was momentarily distracted by one of the deeply important philosophical questions of all time: If you had to give up one of your senses, which one would you part with?

We've all played that game, and my guess is that 99 percent of us would say smell. Oh, we'd toy for a while with the possibility of abandoning taste because that fades a bit with the years anyway. But then an unbidden remembrance of pralines and cream at the ice cream store quickly switches us back to smell.

I was thinking as I walked that perhaps giving up smell wouldn't be an unbearable loss when all of a sudden, as if in answer to that thought, I smelled spring.

There among the aromas of the first cookouts of the season, the budding trees and fresh-cut grass, I honed in on a more subtle smell. I knew it was spring. What a thrill! And had you asked what it smelled like, I'd have to say a nice pastel green, with a touch of pink.

Bring on the snakes.

Be careful!
There may be deer

Daughter Sarah called from Austin the other week to say she had gotten a summer job.

She'd been worried about finding something because, thanks to her trip home for Father's Day, she missed out on the June listings—not to mention the fact that the University of Texas had dumped about 90,000 students on the streets when the semester ended. Odds were good a fair number of those were job hunting.

From the *Richmond Times-Dispatch*, July 15, 2005

But a job had turned up for her. "A great job, Dad. I go to work at 5 a.m. and get off at 11, so I have my afternoons free."

And her dad is thinking, "Ah, she's going to be waitressing on the breakfast shift at the Lady Bird Diner. A good safe job. Or perhaps hostessing or taking cash in a nice hotel restaurant."

"That's great, darling," I say. "What will you be doing?"

"I'll be delivering falafels to supermarkets all over Austin," she replies.

Falafels? Falafels? I've heard of falafels. But what are falafels? Some kind of bread maybe? I don't ask. Rather than let her know I don't know what falafels are, I say, "That's good. Falafels, huh?"

With her part of the conversation going on in one direction, my dad brain is moving in another, touching on the fears we all have for our children. I'm dimly aware of her saying, no, she would not be driving her own car but "a big refrigerated truck."

Her dad is thinking, in what kinds of neighborhoods will my 24-year-old daughter be driving a big refrigerated truck at 5 in the morning? And to whom will she be delivering these falafels? And why isn't she hosting in a nice restaurant?

You can't say those things, you know, when your child is 24. Besides, Barb told me once that parents tell their daughters to "be careful" about 100 more times every year than they do their sons. Not good.

I pretend enthusiasm for her job. It's temporary. In August she'll be back in grad school, working on a master's in creative writing. She may get some good stories out of this job, as I did from driving a Pepsi truck one summer.

Sarah moved to Austin last September to establish Texas residency and qualify for in-state tuition. Though she immediately fell in love with the city, finding a job was difficult. She earned money as a substitute teacher.

On the Road Again

"Do you like that?" I once asked.

"Yes," she had said. "Except for the water balloons."

Sarah is an independent sort, and when she's in Texas, she refuses to take financial help from us. (When she's at home, it's a different matter.) So Barb and I spend time all winter worrying whether she has enough money to pay rent and buy food. Somehow, she gets by.

I shouldn't be surprised at the image of my 115-pound little girl driving a big refrigerated truck. During her year in AmeriCorps after college, she drove the team van all over the country as they built houses for Habitat for Humanity and worked at wild-animal preserves. Her last trip home, she arrived in a borrowed pickup and then drove it into the boonies of Georgia to visit an old boyfriend on her way back.

"How heavy are falafels?" I ask.

"They're sandwiches, Dad. How heavy can they be? Besides, I have a hand truck."

Ah, sandwiches. Of course. That's what falafels are. I look the word up later and find that falafels are sandwiches made of spiced chickpeas and fava beans, Mediterranean in origin.

She calls back yesterday. "Guess what was at the back door of one of the stores I delivered to this morning?" she asks.

Her dad is thinking, Holdup men? Truck-jackers? A crack team of crack addicts? I don't know Austin. Could be anything.

"Two deer," she says. "Just grazing in the grass at the back door of the supermarket. Right downtown. And this guy who was also delivering something went right up and petted them. It was amazing."

"This is a neat job," she adds. "Only six hours a day, $8 an hour, and all the falafels I can eat. And a deer on the doorstep."

I smile. Her dad had almost forgotten how great it was to be young.

Midlife Motorcycle Crisis

When I turned 55 recently, it was a great comfort to me to know that I didn't have to worry about arranging for my midlife crisis because I had already had one, thank you very much, a few years back.

That was actually pretty good planning. I think everybody should just go ahead right now and get that old midlife crisis thing out of the way before you're so old you look absolutely ridiculous doing it, whatever "it" may turn out to be. Then you don't have to worry about walking past a mirror one day when you're 55 and suddenly seeing yourself wearing a T-shirt that says, "No Fear," accompanied by an 18-year-old Lolita with a nose ring, on your way to introduce her to your boss.

Actually, I had my midlife crisis so long ago it's a distant memory, but I do recall that it came in my early 30s, shocked my friends and dismayed my family—and that it was a whole lot of fun.

I don't know how you're planning to celebrate your midlife crisis—that's entirely your business—but I chose to celebrate mine by buying a motorcycle. To that point, never once in my life had I wanted a motorcycle.

But events conspired to bring the odd motorcycle to my attention, and before I knew what I was doing (as is always true of men in midlife crisis mode), I had made a foolhardy move that would change my life for most of a year.

The movie "Easy Rider" was hot on the circuit around that time, and the image of Peter Fonda setting out across America really captured my fancy. The freedom of the

Randy in his "cool" days with his purple Yamaha, 1971.

open road beckoned, as did the chance to feel the wind in my hair while I still had some.

That summer, Barb and I had driven to Athens, Ohio, to visit a couple of friends who were in grad school at Ohio University and, lo, they had just purchased a sweet little Kawasaki to get themselves around campus. For a week, I drove that baby all over town, Barb perched fetchingly on the seat behind me. When we got back to Virginia, we promptly sold our Oldsmobile 98 and bought a Yamaha 200.

For those of you who have always thought a Yamaha 200 was a harmonica, let me assure you that you are not far wrong. That there is a very small motorcycle, one that gives its owners superiority only over the drivers of Big Wheels and Vespas.

It was beautiful. It was shiny bright purple. We drove it for nearly a year as our only mode of transportation. That was one of the years I was writing my dissertation, and our only source of income was substitute teaching. Some days Barb would get called in, some days I would, and no sub-

159

stitute teachers ever got more respect than we did when we arrived at a school on our motorcycle.

Soon Earl, my brother-in-law, along with my young nephew, Steve, and two other good friends all purchased motorcycles, and the six of us would go out together on weekends and zoom around the back roads of Cobham and Boyd Tavern. Eventually, like a bunch of kids, we fancied ourselves a gang and gave the gang a name: the Cismont Sidewinders. We packed lunches in our saddlebags and headed to the mountains. We roared off to Orange for no better reason than to visit the Dairy Queen. I don't think I've had more plain old delightful fun since I was 11 years old.

Then it was over. One night, Barb and I took our bike to Louisa, just to enjoy a beautiful evening on the road. Coming back, on a dark, winding, two-lane blacktop with no broken lines for passing, a Greyhound bus came up behind us. It showed no mercy. It literally rode our back tire for almost 10 miles, so close I couldn't slow down enough to get off the highway. Barb said later she felt that if she had just extended her arm behind her, she would have touched its radiator.

By the time it let up and gave us a chance to just get off the road, we were both screaming out loud in fear. We went home, parked the bike, and to this day the hulk of it remains in a field, where the honeysuckle has grown up around it and time and the elements have taken their toll.

Most of the time I don't even think of its being there, but I did this past Saturday, on one of those days when you just know spring is out there waiting for you. On a drive heading west, Barb and I saw a group of thirty-somethings out on their motorcycles, revving along Interstate 64, their whooping and singing drowned out by the roar of their engines. They looked so pleased with themselves, so free, so unlike the rest of us metal-encased, seat-belted, harnessed-back, middle-aged plodders.

Barb looked across at me and voiced exactly the words I was thinking: "You know," she said, "we must have been stark, raving mad."

160

Keeping Up with the Lexus

*E*arlier this year Dave, a relative by marriage, sold us his 1995 Lexus LS400 for a song. He loved that car, had taken obsessive care of it, changed the oil more often than necessary and kept it ding-free for all those years. I think he sold it for so little money because he couldn't bear to turn it over to a stranger.

Barb and I really didn't need another car, but who turns down a Lexus for a song?

I've been driving it to work every day, and I have to say it's a fine car indeed. I don't mind that it's old or that it has 200,000 miles on it. It has real leather upholstery, folks.

But there are problems that come with driving a Lexus that are not encountered when driving a Mercury or an Olds. Expectations are . . . higher. For instance, when I went to the DMV to get the title changed over, get the plates and so forth, the lady behind the counter didn't seem to believe me when I told her how little we'd paid.

"Do you have a notarized statement from the seller attesting to that selling price?" she asked.

Well, no, I didn't. It never occurred to me that I'd need one.

"Then I have to record the Blue Book price for it," she said, "and you'll have to pay taxes on that higher amount rather than [and here I think I saw her lip curl a bit] the amount you say you paid."

Because Dave lives in another state (and because everybody knows you never turn away from the window at the

DMV once you finally get up there), I just paid the extra tax and went home.

A few days later Barb drove the Lexus to the grocery store. On the way home, she stopped at a stoplight where a seemingly able-bodied man was holding up a sign that said, "Will work for food." She handed him an apple and a banana from her grocery bag, and as the light changed, he yelled after her accusingly, "Nice car, lady."

And it is, except for a small tear in the passenger-side seat. Don't take a Lexus into a shop to get some little thing fixed, though. Just don't do it. Barb stopped by a place where we've had several small repairs made quite reasonably on car seats, but this time she came home breathing hard.

"They wanted $400," she said. "Get me duct tape and a needle and thread."

The first time I took the Lexus to get gas, I was about to place the nozzle in the tank when I noticed a warning on the inside of the little gas tank door that said, "High-test gas only." I've never owned a car that required high-test gas. That was when I knew for sure we were out of our league here. When I told Barb, she grumbled, "Yeah, and I suppose it takes extra-virgin oil, too."

Actually, we're both quite fond of this car. Over the years Barb has always given our cars names, and it took four days for her to bestow a moniker on this one. "This is Alexis," she announced, naming the car after the sexy character Joan Collins used to play on "Dynasty."

"Alexis is the right name because this baby has a lot of miles on her," Barb said, "yet she still turns heads when she comes down the street."

Yep, Alexis it is—and she's got a few nips and tucks in her upholstery to prove it.

It Was Willie

You know how it goes—it's probably happened to you, too. You make your hotel reservations well in advance, you might even specify the room you want, you guarantee it with your credit card, and when you get there, your room has been given to someone else.

That's what happened to Barb and me recently on our first vacation night on the road, passing through Nashville. We were traveling with Barb's sister, Betty, and her husband, Clarence, and we had all agreed to splurge and share the costs of a penthouse apartment for our one evening in Nashville.

But when we arrived in Music City around 9 p.m., the woman at the front desk informed us sheepishly that she had just given the penthouse away to another traveler. We protested, but she said the inn had overbooked, and then she gave us two lovely rooms in another part of the complex.

The next morning on our way to breakfast, we figured out instantly what had happened. There, parked in front of the penthouse that should have been ours, was a magnificent bus, huge, hand-painted and designated in flowery cursive as "Honeysuckle Rose II."

It was Willie. Had to be. And sure enough, as we crossed the parking lot, here came Willie Nelson, striding to breakfast with a friend, deep in conversation.

There are some superstars you wouldn't dare yell out to. You just don't shout, "Hey, Jackie O" across a parking

Details from columns in the *Richmond Times-Dispatch*, September 1, 1993, and June 30, 2003 lot. But in this case I didn't hesitate: "WILLIE!" And Willie stopped in midsentence, whirled around and broke into a grin just as though some rube in Bermuda shorts from Richmond, Va., had not just interrupted his conversation and his progress on the way to breakfast.

He was great. He chatted. He posed for Barb's camera. He suffered the attentions of a couple of other tourists just as obnoxious as we were, and only when everybody had gotten pictures did he and his buddy head on toward the restaurant.

It was when I got back to our car that I realized the guy with Willie had been the talented country singer outlaw David Allan Coe. (Among his hits were "You Never Even Call Me by My Name" and "Mona Lisa Lost Her Smile." Coe also wrote the classic lyrics to "Take This Job and Shove It.") I was sorry I hadn't recognized him because I've always enjoyed his music—and possibly he was sorry, too. Either he was unhappy that his stroll to breakfast had been interrupted or he was unhappy to have been unrecognized, because when we had Barb's picture developed, there I was with Willie, and David Allan Coe standing directly behind, his finger very pointedly up his nose.

(For the record: A Google search now makes it clear that this was not Mr. Coe's first use of what we might call the outlaw's salute. Nor was it his last.)

Willie and Randy ... and a salute from David Allan Coe

BARB: *For almost 30 years, Randy has been reporting on our annual August trip to the Old Fiddler's Convention in Galax, Va., and our modest but magnificent accommodations for that week at a cabin in nearby Mouth of Wilson. Two years ago, in order to be close to medical facilities should we need them, we finally gave up the isolated mountain cabin and moved into Galax for the week, this time in a log cabin on the river. There's no bad place for bluegrass!*

Our Little Cabin Home in Galax

*E*ach morning around 6, the gray mist sweeps across the top of the mountain in distant puffs, like the ghosts of Confederate dead marching home again.

It rolls down over the miles and miles of trees in a

From the *Richmond Times-Dispatch*, August 18, 1999

matter of seconds, finally forming an impenetrable, colorless curtain of fog that hangs, sky to earth, at the bottom of the field just in front of our cabin.

Barb and I are back in Grayson County, still my choice as Virginia's most beautiful spot, this year to enjoy the 64th gathering of the Old Fiddlers Convention in Galax.

This is the most soothing, relaxing week of our entire year. Barb says her very soul is quieted by the sight of these hills, the sounds of this simple and lively music, the taste of clean mountain air, the feel of an always-cool breeze blowing in the loft window.

On our first night back at the little log cabin hanging high off a ridge about 30 miles from Galax, I stepped out on the porch to check for tomorrow's weather and immediately lost my breath. The stars, which at our Richmond home generally are lost to city lights, here filled the sky. There were thousands, in clusters so thick that separating out even the Big Dipper was nearly impossible.

I felt my way back to the door in the darkness and urged Barb and our friend Hattie Palmer, the other early arrival for festival week, to come outside and look.

As we stood, rendered silent by the spectacle, we heard just to our left a loud and serious-sounding growl that sent us scrambling for the door. The owner of the cabin, a wiry mountain man who lives down in the hollow, had mentioned once that this is the area where bears found roaming in towns all across the state are brought to be released. We always keep that in mind.

The blackberries along the lane bloomed for us this year, arriving later in the cool mountains than they do in the rest of the state. We picked some for breakfast, which—no matter how good our intentions—escalates in quantity in the mountain air. There are thick cakes of sausage, platters of eggs and bacon, slow-cooked grits, toast piled high and juicy slices of home-grown tomatoes. Though our activity consists of driving the winding roads into Galax for the music each day, serious fortifications for the trip always seem in order.

I write each year about the joys of this Galax experience and how everyone we bring along with us loves the cabin, the mountains and the people even if they don't know much about bluegrass.

Our friend Sarah Dowdey is a first-timer this year. Her music of choice is opera, but she—a talented photographer—arrived with her camera ready to capture the amazing faces in the crowd: the rail-thin mountain women in long flowing dresses, men with hair and beards to the waist, shy children who make music onstage like seasoned veterans, and everywhere, a character. A favorite regular is "Duck Man," who comes each year carrying a ceramic duck in his arms because, he tells us, it's a great conversation piece. People find it hard to resist asking, "What's with the duck?"

By Friday and Saturday nights, the crowd is huge, with people packed so thick in folding chairs in front of the stage that procuring an elephant ear is a slow process. But folks are patient and peaceful. This is our eighth year, and we've never heard an unpleasant word exchanged here. How many places can you go where people walk around for a week with smiles on their faces?

There is such joy in this music, such pride and tradition. Strangers step onto plywood boards scattered here and there, to clog dance together, faces radiant, feet flying, heads bobbing up and down above the crowd of fans in their folding chairs. Whole families come together to share tunes they've played over and over in their own living rooms on dulcimer, fiddle, banjo and mandolin.

On Sunday morning, our last day in the cabin, Barb rousted me and our overnight friends to watch the sun rise over the mountain. She went from bed to bed, insisting we all get up.

"Grab your quilt," she said as she shook me alive from some beautiful dream. I remember grumbling from be-

SARAH DOWDEY
Barb, Randy and friends Hattie Palmer and Gerry Wells
wake up for the sunrise at the Galax cabin.

neath my warm covers, "Why are you doing this?"

I soon found out. Sitting on the front porch, wrapped head to toe in my quilt, I watched nature's grandest everyday spectacle.

The mist once again rolled over the mountain, formed its thick gray wall and dropped low in the valley below. Then the sky along the ridge turned pale yellow and streaked pink until in an instant the entire sun appeared as though hoisted high by the strongest of invisible hands.

Friend Sarah was so inspired she burst into "Break Forth O Beauteous Heavenly Light," and complaints about the early hour ceased. We all grew quiet. Galax was over, except for the memories we always take home from this glorious annual experience.

FLIGHTS OF FANCY